Reading Workbook C

Siegfried Engelmann
Owen Engelmann
Karen Davis

Acknowledgments

The authors are grateful to the following people for their assistance in the preparations of Reading Mastery Transformations Grade K Reading.

Blake Engelmann
Charlene Tolles-Engelmann
Cally Dwyer
Toni Reeves

We'd also like to acknowledge, from McGraw Hill, the valuable contributions by:

Mary Eisele
Nancy Stigers
Jason Yanok

mheducation.com/prek-12

Copyright © 2021 McGraw-Hill Education

All rights reserved. No part of this publication may be reproduced or distributed in any form or by any means, or stored in a database or retrieval system, without the prior written consent of McGraw-Hill Education, including, but not limited to, network storage or transmission, or broadcast for distance learning.

Permission is granted to reproduce the material contained on Mastery Tests 12–16, Sides 1 and 2, on the condition that such material be reproduced only for classroom use; be provided to students, teachers, or families without charge; and be used solely in conjunction with *Reading Mastery Transformations*.

Send all inquiries to:
McGraw-Hill Education
8787 Orion Place
Columbus, OH 43240

ISBN: 978-0-07-905551-4
MHID: 0-07-905551-6

Printed in the United States of America.

5 6 7 8 9 10 LON 28 27 26 25

My name is _____.

1. Bob had to be home by ▆.
   • 2 • 3 • five • nine

2. Did Bob make it home by five? ____

3. A man said, "I see a hill of mud that can ▆."
   • fly • sit • eat • run

4. His dad said, "But you didn't ▆ the path."
   • stay in • stay near
   • sit in   • sleep near

5. Can Bob hike with his pals for some time? ____

My name is _____.

1. We can hike and we can ▬.
   • sit   • eat   • bike   • sleep

2. Do we bike to the sea in the rain?
   _____

3. We bike to the sea if it ▬.
   • is cold   • rains   • snows   • is dry

4. Do we come home with tales? _____

5. Do we come home with tails? _____

6. We come home with tales of ▬.
   • stones   • seeds   • stoves   • sails
   • stores   • sea   • piles   • waves

Side 1

hole rode **road** roads	seal sees sail **sea**
weeds jump **grass** ants	**roads** road rode paths
greet mile smiles smile	seed see **sea** seas

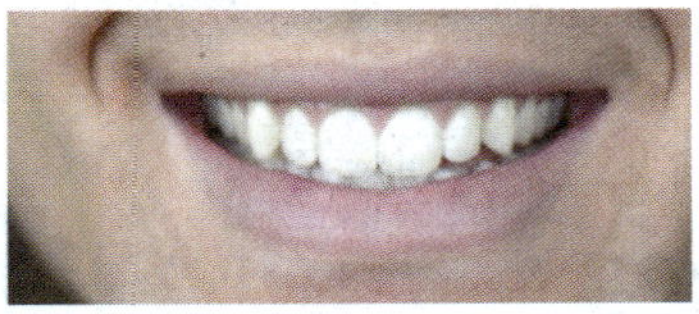

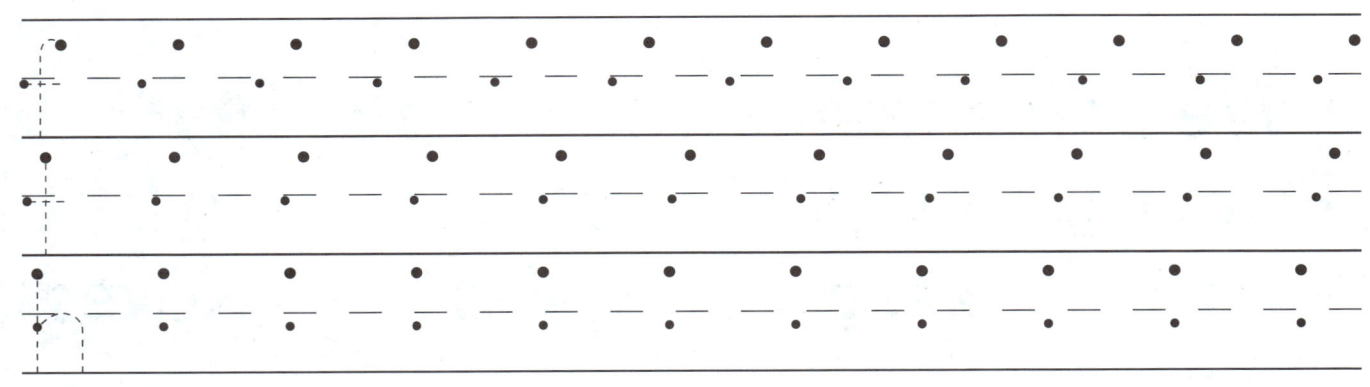

Side 2

My name is _____.

1. The other day, we rode to a ▮.
   - sea
   - lake
   - hill
   - cave

2. We ▮.
   - ate
   - filled pails
   - sold games
   - told tales
   - played games
   - made kites

3. The gear was near a ▮.
   - stove
   - hill
   - hive
   - hat

4. I have a sore ▮.
   - hear
   - rear
   - gear
   - tear
   - nose
   - bike
   - ear
   - wheel

5. Can Ann hear? _____

6. Can Ann sit? _____

7. The note is from ▮.
   - Dan
   - Fran
   - Ann
   - an

Side 1

goat
goats
ram
rams

tale
tales
tail
tails

hide
have
hive
hole

tale
tail
tails
store

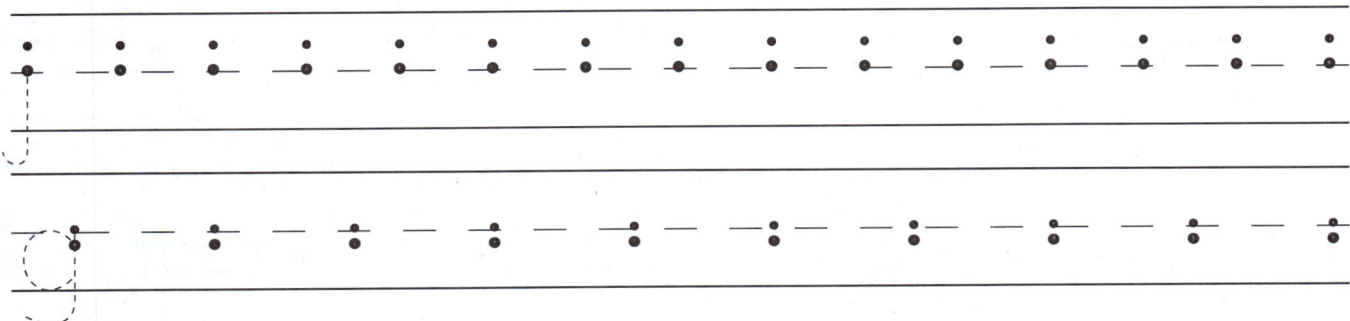

note   notes   sick   crow   crows

Side 2

My name is _____.

- This is my home.

- He dug a hole into the home.

- He ate a bug.

- And I can eat bugs if I feel like it.

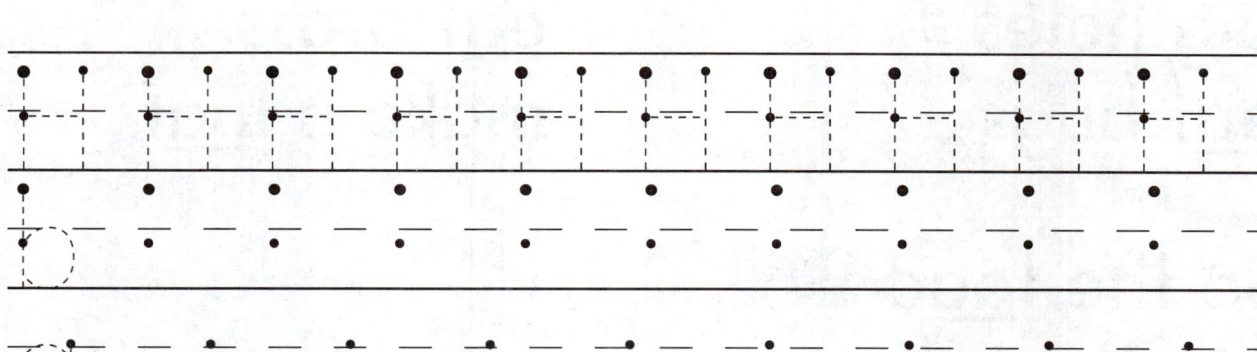

Side 1

1. I had you read a tale of a ▇.
   - mean ram
   - mean bug
   - rat
   - fine home
   - fine hill
   - toad

2. Did the toad like holes in his home?
   _____
   _ _ _ _
   _____

3. The bug said, "I can make ▇ if I feel like it."
   - homes
   - hill
   - hills
   - holes

4. The toad said, "I can ▇ if I feel like it."
   - dig holes
   - eat grass
   - eat bugs
   - make a loaf

5. So the toad ▇.
   - ate the bug
   - ran into a pal
   - sat in the grass
   - dug a hole

Side 2

My name is _____.

1. I hate to ▆▆.
 • sleep • wait • run • play

2. I have to sit ▆▆.
 • in a van • by my home • and wait
 • by a lake • in the rain • and sleep

3. I wait for ▆▆.
 • my pal • a cat • the sun • a meal

4. Is my pal late? _____

5. At last I ▆▆ him.
 • feel • see • kiss
 • lick • kick • hear

6. We will have some ▆▆.
 • sun • sleep • grass • fun

Side 1

		stone
_____	_____	stones
		pig
		pigs
		pile
_____	_____	piles
		cave
		caves

play   pal   hive   (pals)   ~~hive~~
pals   have   pill   4   3
hike   pal   hide   pals   hiked
hive   hill   hive   hits   plays
hid   have   pals   pal   hills
hid   play   hike   pals   have

u

n

Side 2

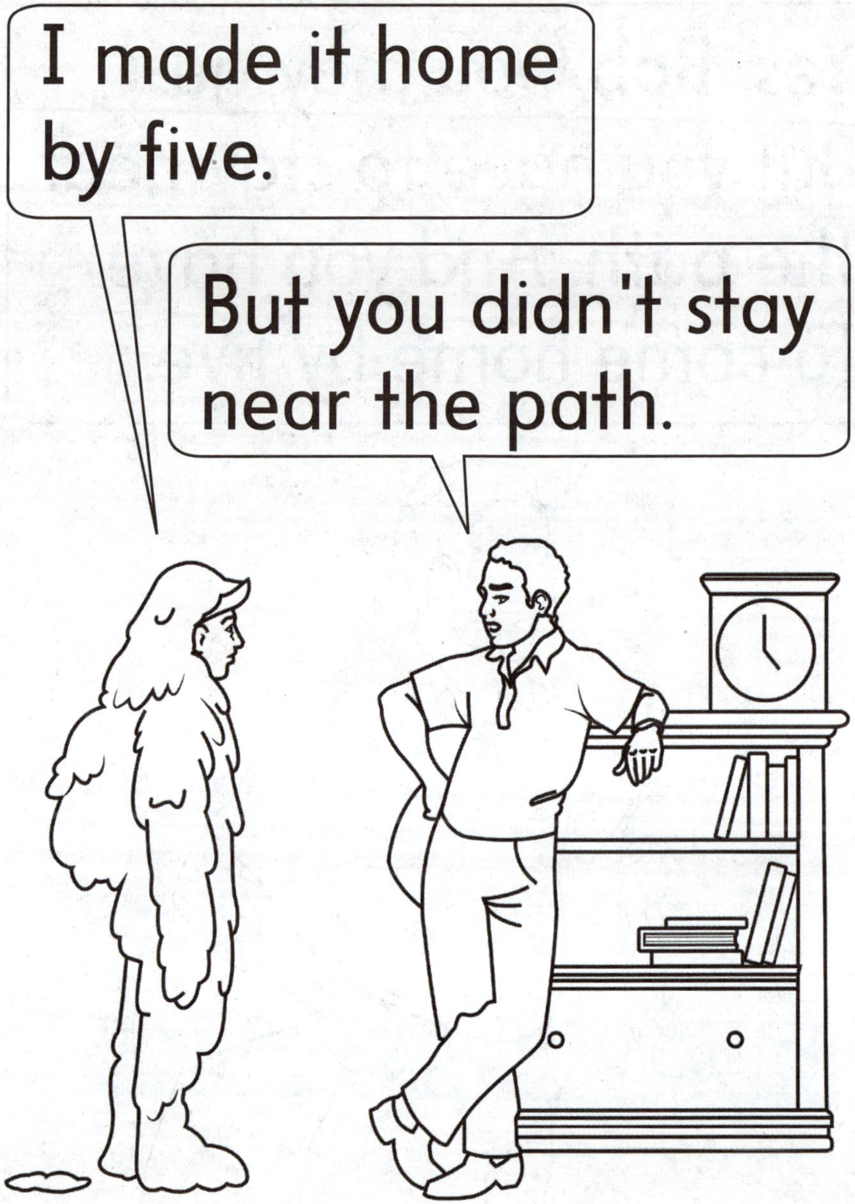
I made it home by five.
But you didn't stay near the path.

fold

Bob
The Hill of Mud

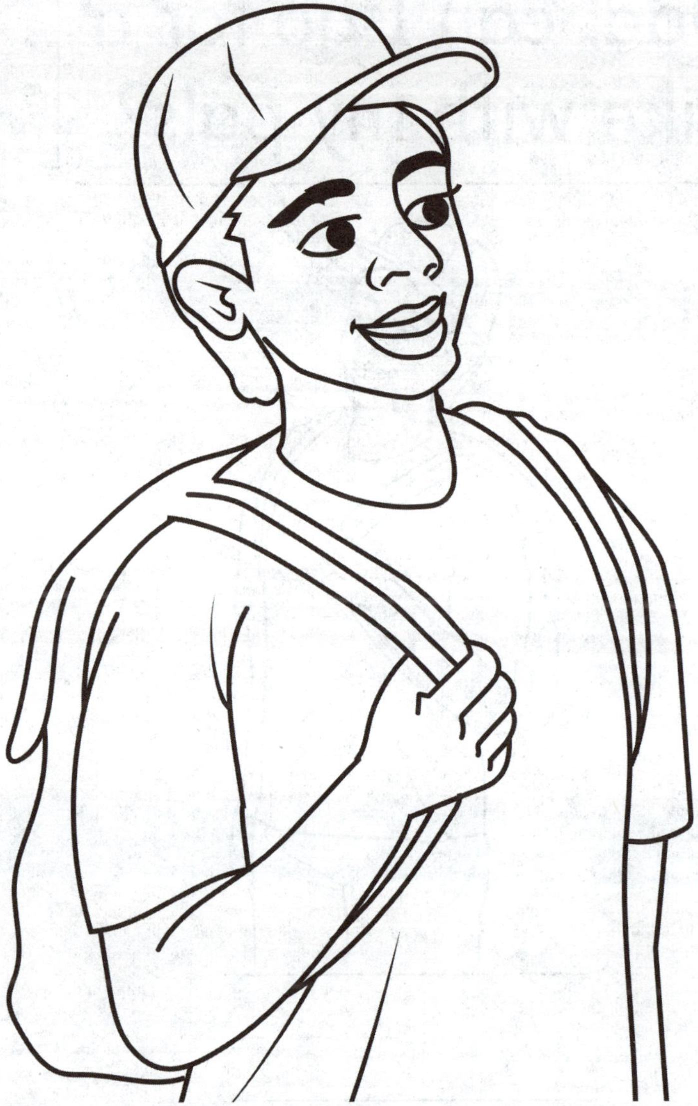

Yes, Bob, you may go. But you have to stay near the path. And you have to come home by five.

Dad, can I go for a hike with my pals?

My name is _____.

1. We pl<u>ay</u>ed ▉.
   - in sno<u>w</u>
   - with a stick
   - near a mol<u>e</u>
   - in the r<u>ai</u>n
   - with a dim<u>e</u>
   - in the sun

2. We at<u>e</u> ▉.
   - n<u>ea</u>r the stov<u>e</u>
   - in a stor<u>e</u>
   - n<u>ea</u>r a ston<u>e</u>
   - in his home
   - in the r<u>ai</u>n
   - in the sun

3. At last I am ▉.
   - m<u>ea</u>n
   - sor<u>e</u>
   - saf<u>e</u>
   - dry

4. I go to the ▉.
   - path
   - sun
   - rug
   - lak<u>e</u>

5. Is it tim<u>e</u> for me to sleep? _____

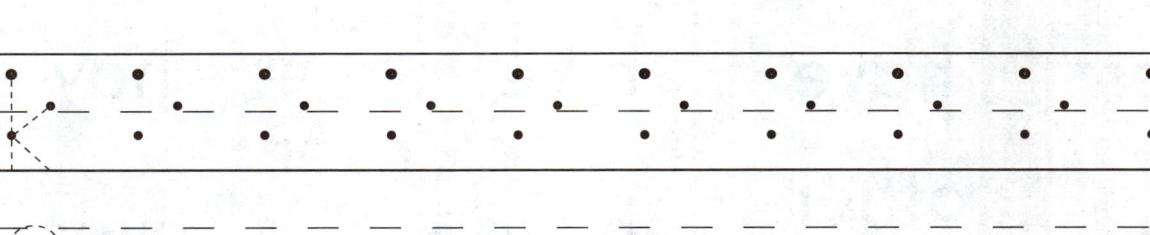

Side 1

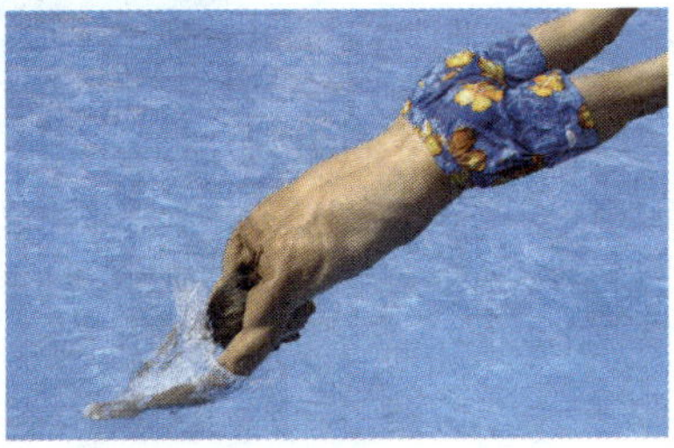

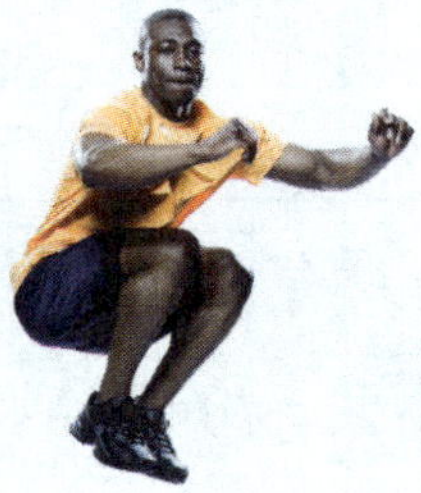

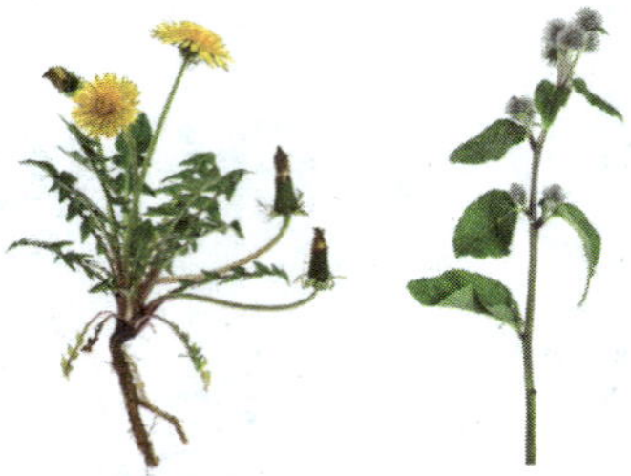

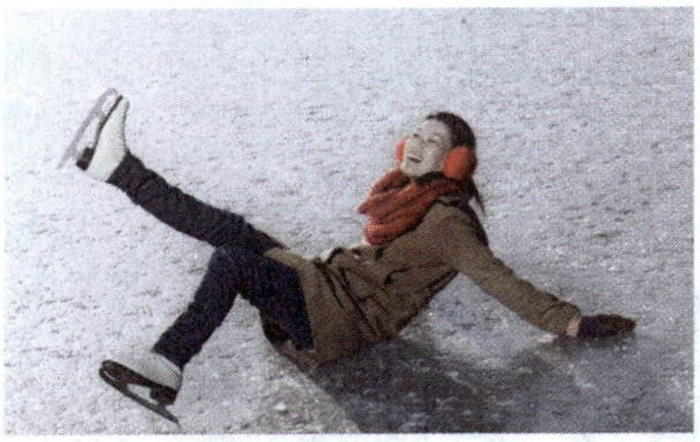

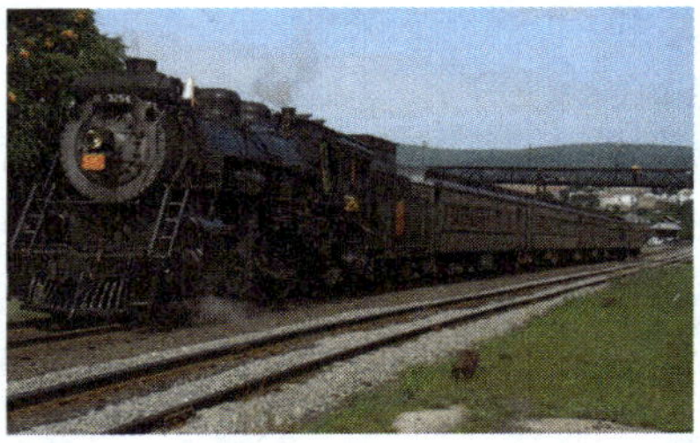

train	jump	slip	weed
trains	three	dive	weeds

have hate has other

other 3 | have 4

over hay hive

the the

have has of

other have hike hay

over

hate other have over

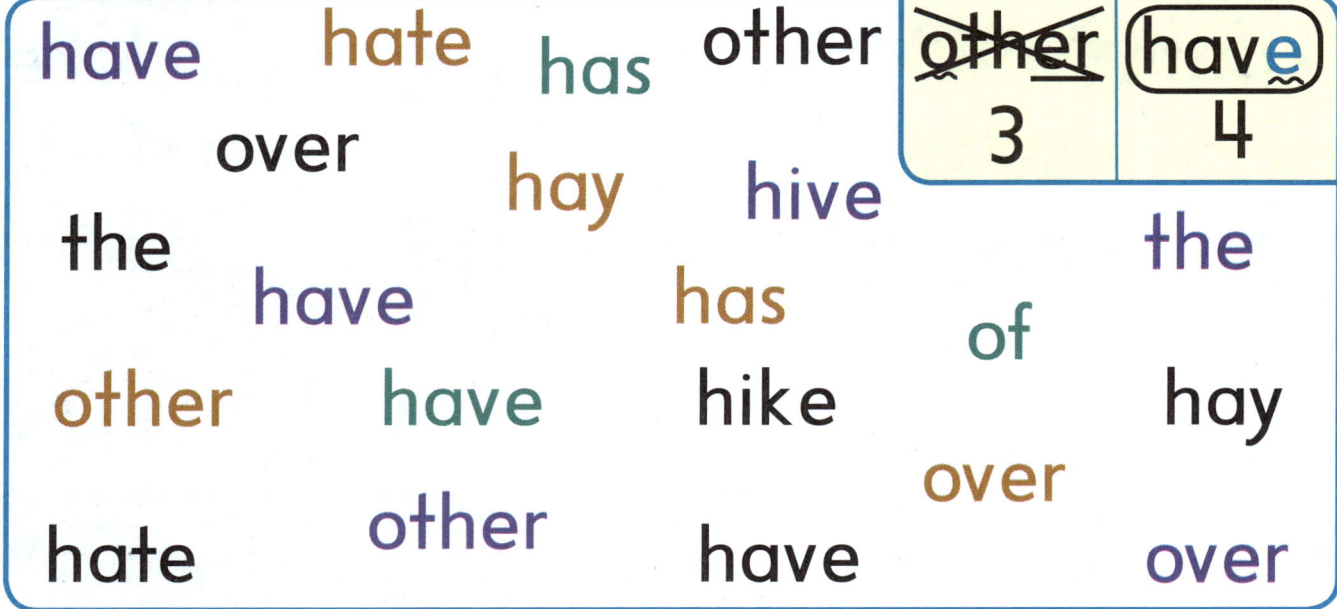

My name is _____.

I will make that fire _____.

We must keep that fire _____ from _____.

f<u>a</u>rm   bad   the   big   b<u>a</u>rn   cold

1. Who made the pals cold?
   • a pig   • a wind   • a cat   • a fire

2. Who made a fire?
   • the wind   • my dad
   • the barn   • the pals

3. Did the wind make the fire big? _____

4. In no time that fire was ▇▇▇.
   • cold   • in the rain
   • near the barn   • by a home

wheel
wheels
hive
hives
soaked
spy

Side 2

My name is _____.

Ho ho. It's time for a _____ _____.

fine   fire   home   b<u>ar</u>n   pals   p<u>ai</u>ls

Side 1

1. The m<u>ea</u>n wind mad<u>e</u> ▇.
   - a bad jok<u>e</u>
   - r<u>ai</u>n
   - a fin<u>e</u> jok<u>e</u>
   - fir<u>e</u> l<u>ea</u>p ov<u>er</u> to a b<u>ar</u>n
   - fir<u>e</u> lick at a b<u>a</u>rn
   - sno<u>w</u>

2. <u>W</u>h<u>o</u> said, "If we don't hold this fir<u>e</u>, the b<u>a</u>rn will go up in flam<u>es</u>"?
   - the wind
   - the pals
   - Bob
   - the fir<u>e</u>

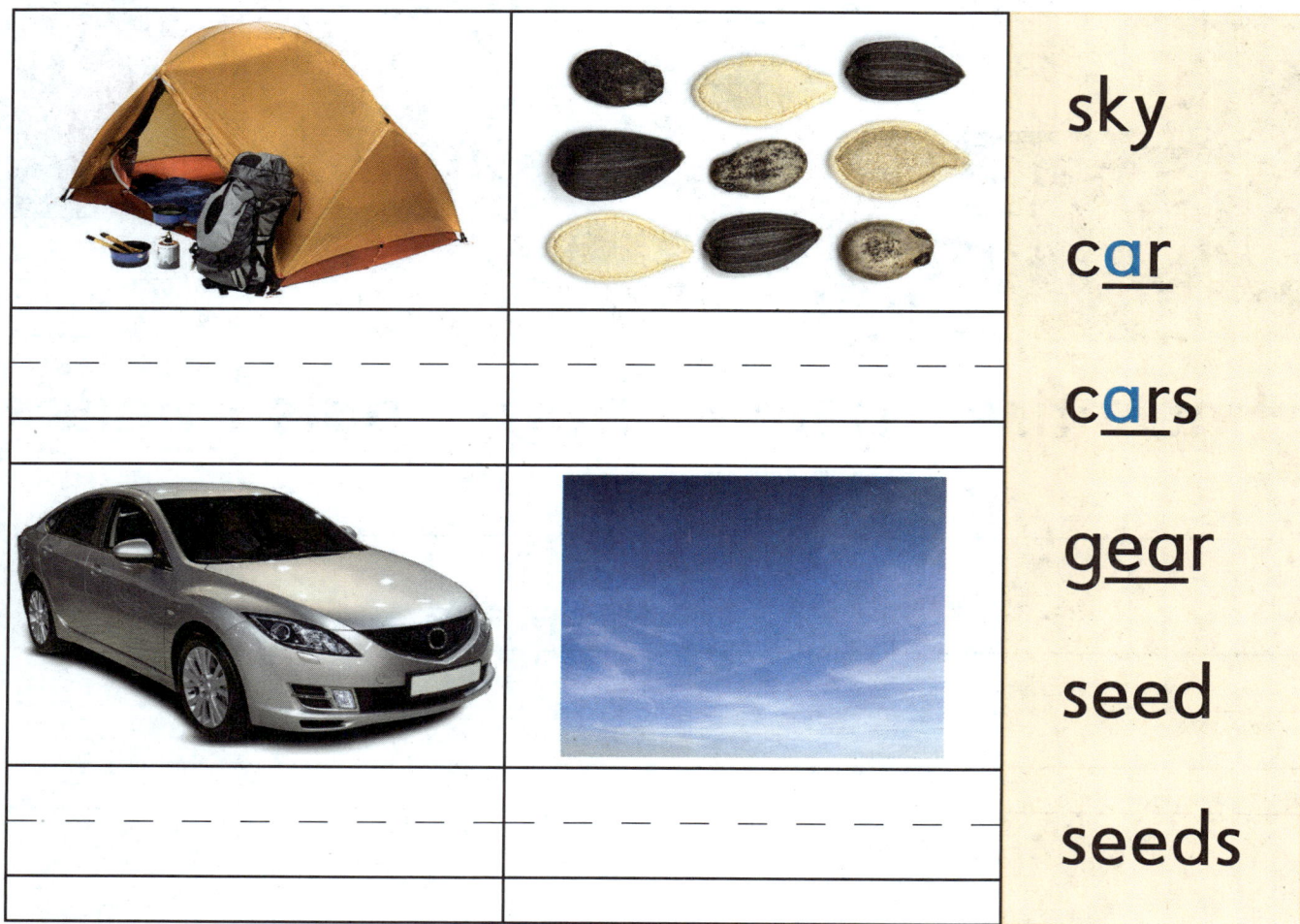

My name is _____.

• ⟵ We like rain.

 • • ⟵ I will keep those flames away from the barn.

 • • ⟵ I will blow big flames up the side of that barn.

• ⟵ I hate rain.

 • • ⟵ Leave this farm or I will soak you some more.

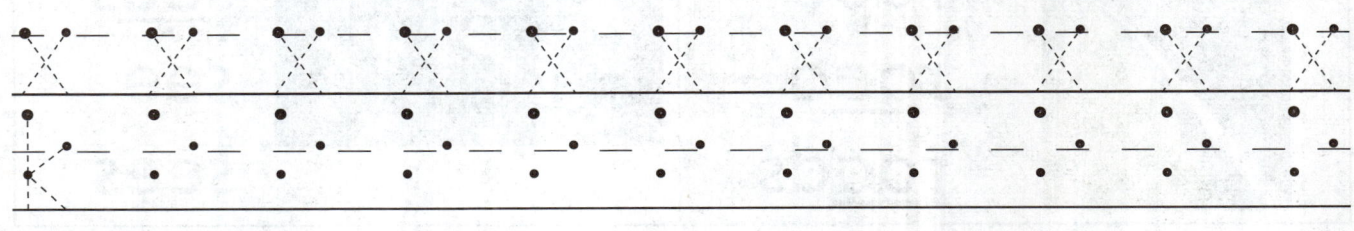

Side 1

1. The mean wind made flames go up the side of ▓▓▓.
   - the barn • a tree • the farm • a hill

2. What came from the sky?
   - the fly • rain • Bob • snow

3. Who said, "We like rain"?
   - the mean wind • the fire
   - the rain • the pals

4. Who said, "I hate rain"?
   - the mean wind • the fire
   - the rain • the pals

rode
rope
road
roads

sea
seas
see
sees

Side 2

My name is _____.

1. _____ 2. _____

3. _____ 4. _____

Ann and some pals rode bikes to a lake. The pals pl<u>ayed</u> games and ate. No hive was n<u>ear</u> the g<u>ear</u>, so Ann is fine.

- -

It is time to eat. We will eat in his home near the stove. At last I am dry. It is time for me to sleep.

fold

My Pal

I hate to wait. But I have to sit and wait while it rains.

Side 1

wh   sh   <u>a</u>r

1. jump
2. don't
3. wind
4. dive

1. hill
2. b<u>ar</u>n
3. while
4. began

1. <u>are</u>
2. who
3. oth<u>er</u>
4. you

I hear him and see him. I will jump up. It is time for us to have some fun.

At last my pal is home. We have fun as we play with a stick and play in the rain.

Side 2

121

My name is _____.

- I hav*e* a rug.
- Hold on.
- I don't like mud.
- We can hav*e* s*o*me fun.
- This rug is fast.
- We can sit on the rug.

Side 1

1. Who slid on the rug?
   - the goat
   - the bug
   - the pig
   - the ram
   - a crow
   - the toad

2. What did the pals sit on?
   - mud
   - a rug
   - a rock
   - a rag

3. The pig said, "Hold ▇▇."
   - a rope
   - my tail
   - a stone
   - on

4. The goat said, "This rug is ▇▇."
   - dry
   - big
   - fast
   - slow

___	___	___

___	___	___

flames   ship   lick   tear   barn
back   ships   tears   barns

Side 2

My name is _____.

- A tree is in the w<u>ay</u>.
- We will miss that tree.
- We can slid<u>e</u> on the mud s<u>o</u>me more.

- The g<u>oa</u>t and I hav<u>e</u> mud on us.
- Oh d<u>ea</u>r.

1. Who said, "A tree is in the way"?
   - mole   • pig   • goat   • ram

2. Who said, "We will miss that tree"?
   - mole   • pig   • goat   • ram

3. Did the pals miss the tree? _____

4. What did the rug run into?
   - a hole   • a rug   • a rock   • a tree

5. What did the pals land in?
   - tree   • grass   • mud   • hay

Side 2

My name is _____.

I will have _____.

Who are _____?

tree   you   mole   fun   some   crow

1. Who dug a hole under a tree?
   - crow   • big one   • mole   • goat

2. What did she run into?
   - hole   • tree   • big two   • crow

3. Who was in the tree?
   - big one   • mole   • goat   • crow

4. The crow said, "▭."
   - Who are you.   • I am the big one.
   - I am stuck.   • I will try.
   - I don't know.   • Oh mole.

car   cars   hive   hives   fin   fins

Side 2

My name is _____.

You dug into the side of my _____.

I need to free these _____.

hole feet mole crow free snake home

1. A crow made a mole think that a tree was ▇.
   - a man
   - a fast rug
   - the big two
   - the big one

2. The mole said, "I dig, dig, dig, but these feet are ▇.
   - big, big, big
   - the big one's
   - old, old, old
   - deep

3. A mole came to the home of a wise ▇.
   - rat
   - snake
   - man
   - crow

4. The snake said, "Why do you dig into my ▇?"
   - tree
   - cave
   - home
   - hill

My name is _____.

1. The ▮ was trying to free the big one.
   - crow • mole • snake • big one

2. The ▮ told the mole that she was digging under a tree.
   - crow • mole • snake • big one

3. Who said, "I think I know what to do"?
   - crow • mole • snake • big one

4. The snake will play ▮.
   - a game • in a lake • with a coat • a joke

be	path	coat
bee	paths	coats
bees	road	cold
bugs	roads	snow
hole	trail	rain
hive	trails	rains

Side 1

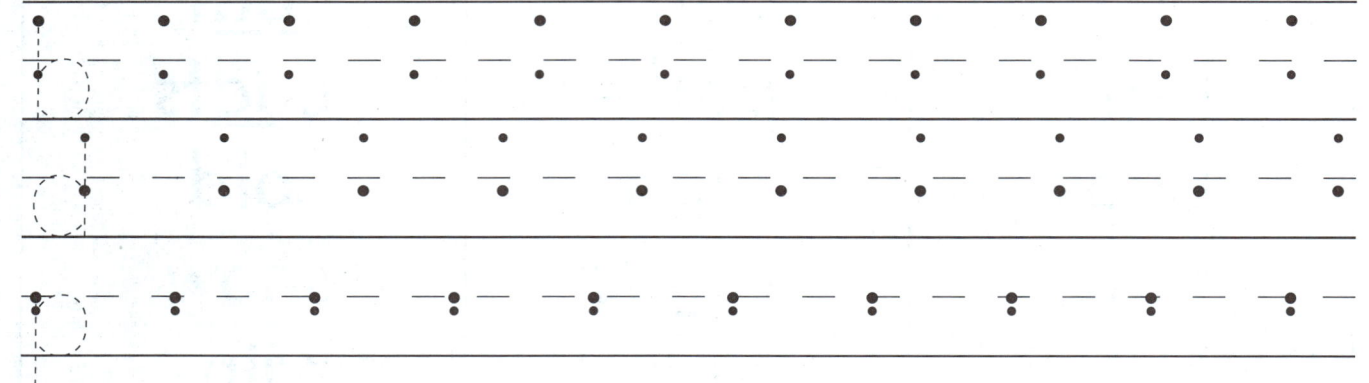

drive   wheel   ship   stove   tail
sing   wheels   ships   stoves   tails

Note to Dad

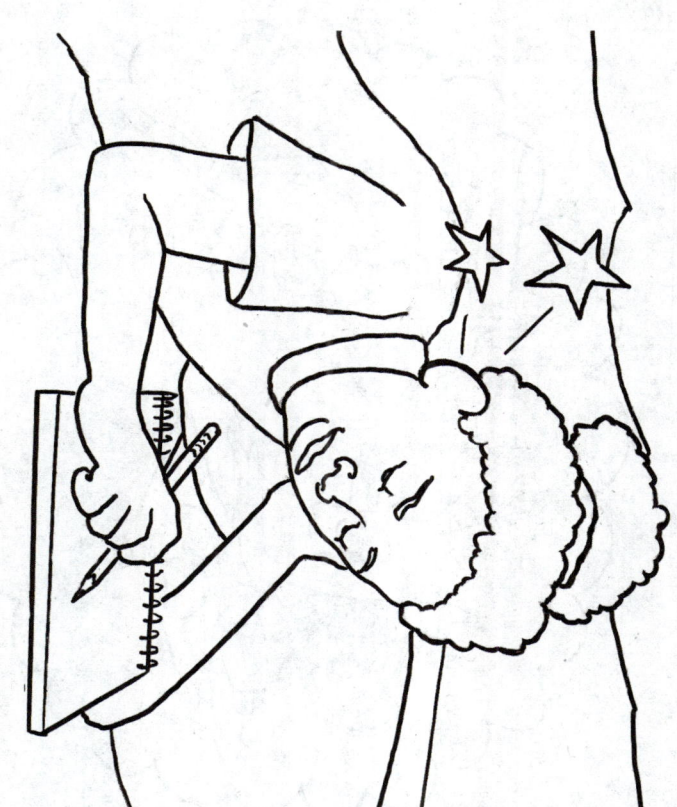

I have a sore ear, but I can hear. And I have a ____ rear. So I can't sit. And I can't ride my bike for a while.

From Ann

Dear Dad,
The other day we rode bikes to a lake. We ate and played games.

I had my gear near a bee hive. Bees gave me some tears.

My name is _____.

1. Who made plans to play a joke on the crow?
   - the mole
   - the crow
   - the snake
   - the tree
   - the big one

2. Who told the crow that the big one was stuck in gold?
   - the snake
   - the big one
   - the tree
   - the mole

3. The crow
   - said, "Ho ho."
   - slid into the hole.
   - said, "Go in the hole."
   - came from the hole.
   - asked, "What did you say?"
   - came to a lump of gold.

4. What did the crow see in the hole?
   - gold
   - cold snow
   - mud
   - the big one

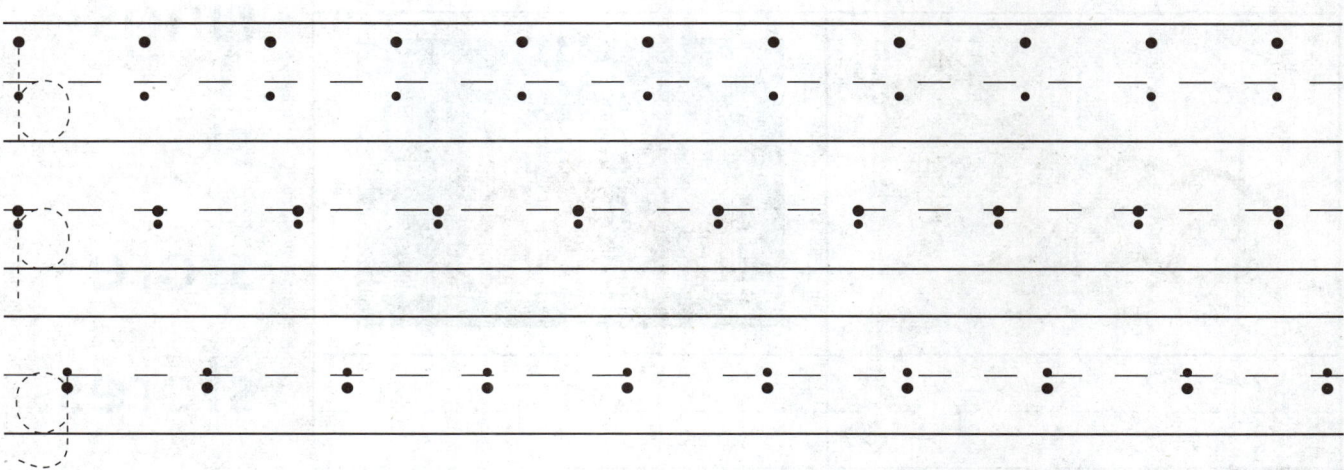

Side 1

for	on
four	two
five	too
three	one

to	tale
too	tales
two	tail
three	tails

barn
barns
ring
rings
sky
store
stores

My name is _____.

You can have the _____.

cold   mole   snake   snow   gold   crow

1. As the crow started to grab for the gold, it became ▓.
   • dark   • big   • old   • cold

2. Did the crow grab a lump of gold? ____

3. Who said, "Shame on you for playing jokes on moles"?
   • mole   • the big one   • snake   • tree

4. Who did the crow think was mad at him?
   • the big one   • mole   • snake   • tree

5. The crow played ▓ more jokes on moles.
   • one   • two   • three   • no

farm   farms   sing   mother   mothers

Side 2

My name is _____.

"Rain, rain, _____."

come
away
Ann
mother
other
Jan
go
here

1. Jan's singing made her mother ▬▬.
   • feel fine   • sick   • sit   • smile

2. Jan asked her mother to ▬▬ with her.
   • stop singing   • eat   • sleep   • sing

3. Jan's mother said," ▬▬ "
   • I sing the same thing.   • Sing with me.
   • I like the way you sing.   • No.
   • Can you sing other things?   • Yes.
   • What can I do for you?

4. Is Jan's mother sick of her singing now? ____

Side 1

 • • A n<u>ai</u>l on some h<u>ay</u>

 • • Trees and a hill of mud

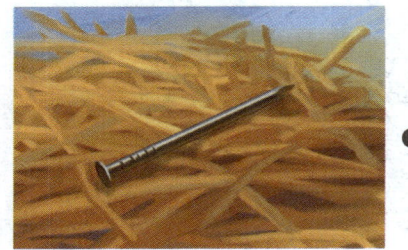 • • Pigs in a b<u>ar</u>n

 • • A cro**w** in the sno**w**

 • • Fiv**e** feet in mud

Side 2

My name is _____.

of
pig
corn
pill
goat
pile
cow

1. Who liked to eat?
   • a crow   • a goat   • three rams
   • two bugs   • a pig   • one snake

2. Who told the pig and the goat to start eating?
   • Bob   • a crow   • a cow   • a snake

3. The cow said, "I think I will ▮▮▮▮."
   • eat too   • eat two   • eat one   • sleep

4. Who ate faster?
   • the pig   • the goat   • the big one   • the cow

5. Who got mad?
   • the pig   • the goat   • the big one   • the cow

Side 1

- A big <u>sh</u>op
- A <u>sh</u>ip and a fi<u>sh</u>
- A bug in a lake
- A fi<u>sh</u> on dry land

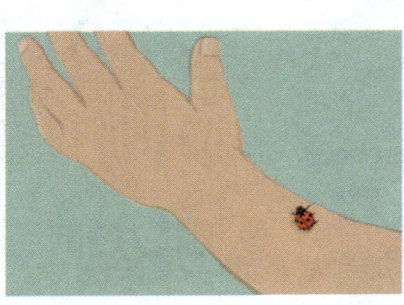

- A bug on an <u>a</u>rm
- A bug in a rug
- Five hands
- Three bugs and four feet

- An ant in the sun
- A bee on a hive
- A bug on an <u>a</u>rm
- A bug in the d<u>a</u>rk

started   leap   those

wheels   over   away

Side 2

My name is _____.

1. _____ 2. _____

3. _____ 4. _____

 o ___ er

- -

1. Who ate more corn?
_____

2. Who ate faster?
_____

3. The goat and the
_____ got mad.

fold

Corn for Three

Side 1

One day, a goat, a cow, and a pig were playing near a pile of corn.
 The goat said, "I can eat that corn."
 The pig said, "Me too."
 The cow said, "I think I will eat too."

---

1. she
2. were
3. started
4. playing

1. got
2. think
3. now
4. under

1. said
2. was
3. what
4. gold

The goat said, "I can eat faster than you."
 The pig said, "You can not."
 A cow said, "Why don't you start eating and see who wins?"
 So the goat and the pig started to eat corn.
 The cow said, "I think I will eat some corn too."

Side 2

My name is _____.

I _____ for my _____.

rain
mail
pal
hat
man
wait

1. Did the sun sh<u>i</u>ne? _____

2. <u>Wh</u>a̰t p<u>ar</u>ts w<u>er</u>ḛ soa<u>ked</u>?
   • wheel • <u>ear</u> • tail • rug • coat • hat

3. <u>Wh</u>a̰t did the pals plan to do?
   • stay dry   • have a m<u>ea</u>l
   • eat corn   • have lots of fun

4. My pal is ▇▇▇.
   • the mail man • a cat • Bob • on time

Side 1

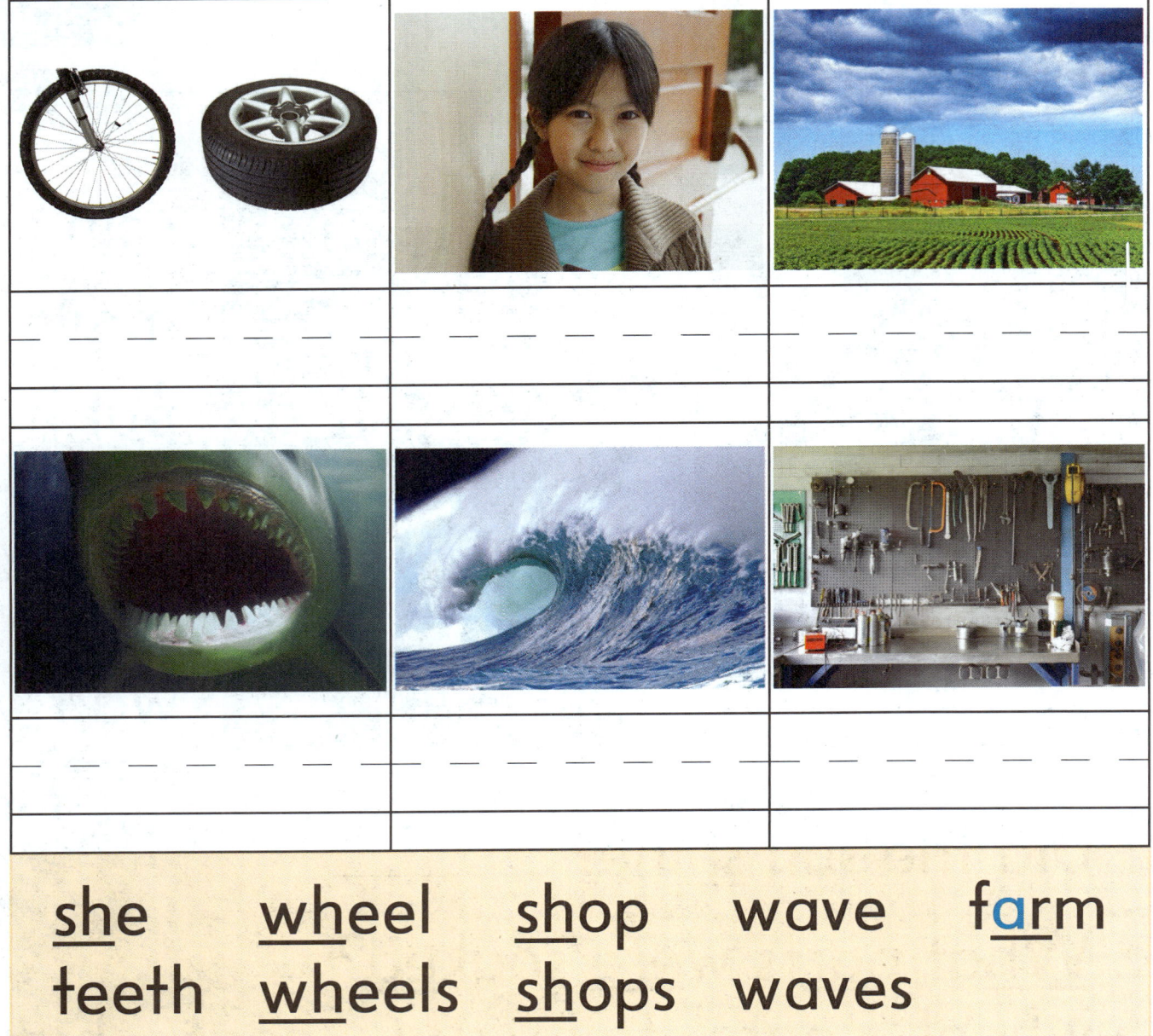

she   wheel   shop   wave   farm
teeth   wheels   shops   waves

this   teeth   coat   wait
read   while   farms   over

Side 2

My name is _____.

1. What did three pals make?
   - a barn
   - a fire
   - a wind
   - a hole

2. Who made flames leap up the barn?
   - Bob
   - the pals
   - the mean wind
   - the rain

3. Who soaked the fire?
   - Bob
   - the pals
   - the mean wind
   - the rain

4. The rain said, "_____"
   - You can't stop this fire.
   - We like rain.
   - I will keep those flames away.
   - I will blow big flames.
   - Leave this farm.
   - I will soak you some more.

goat   away   farm   start
that   what   leave   sailed

Side 1

bee
bees
be
fly

to
too
two
three

tale
tales
tail
tails

sailed
sale
sail
sails

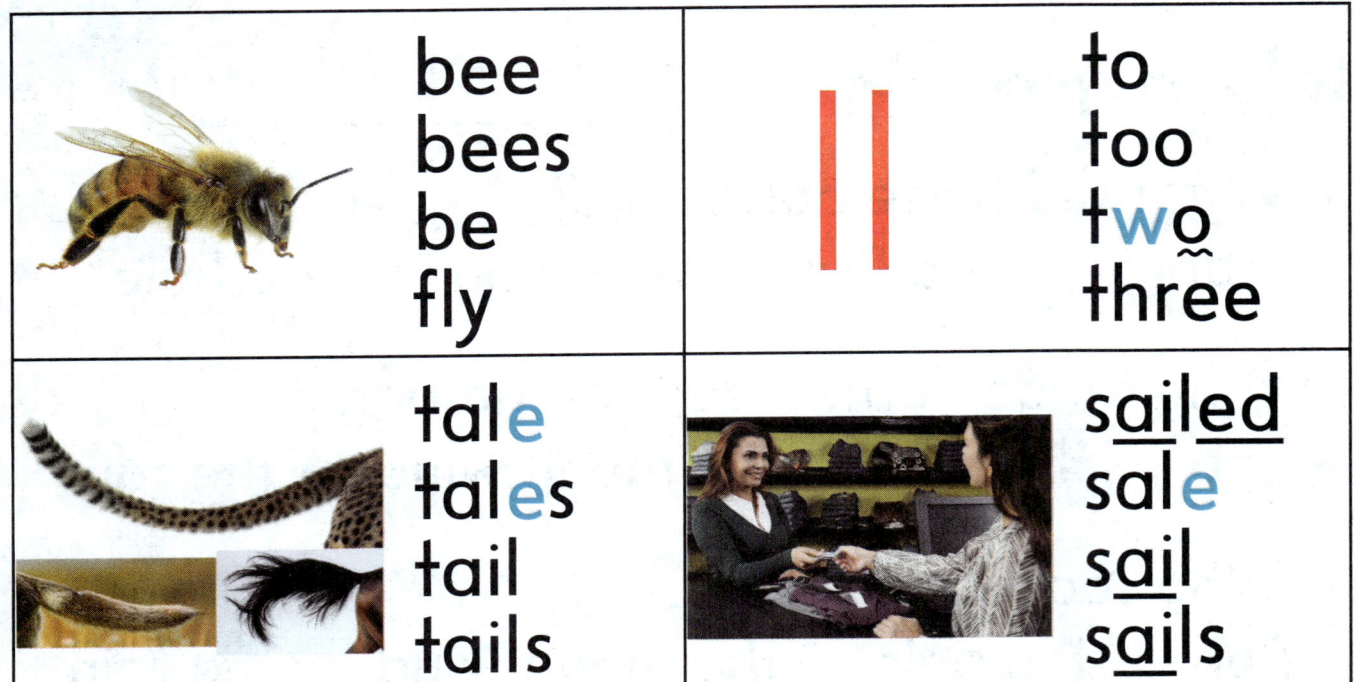

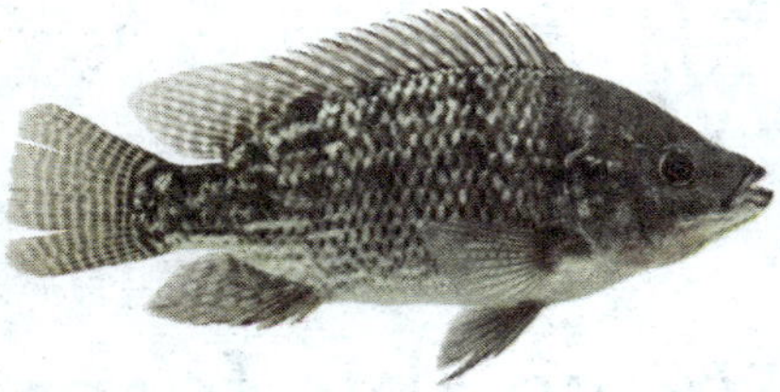

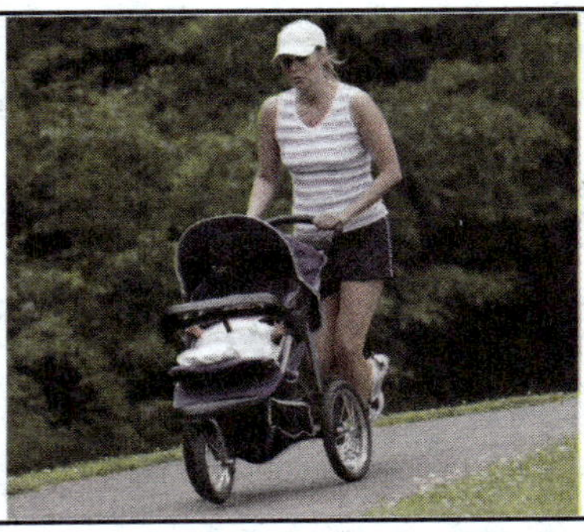

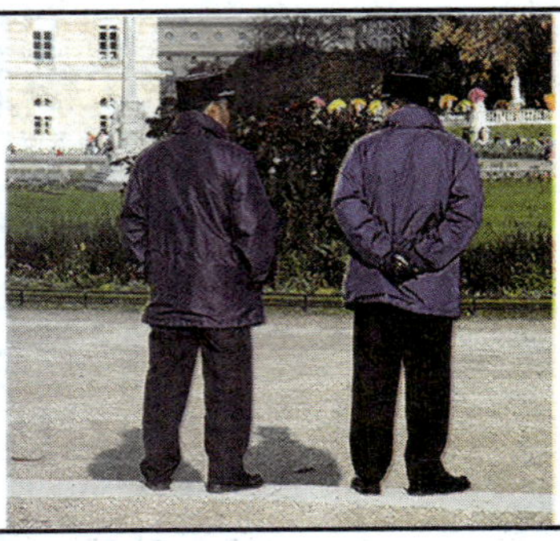

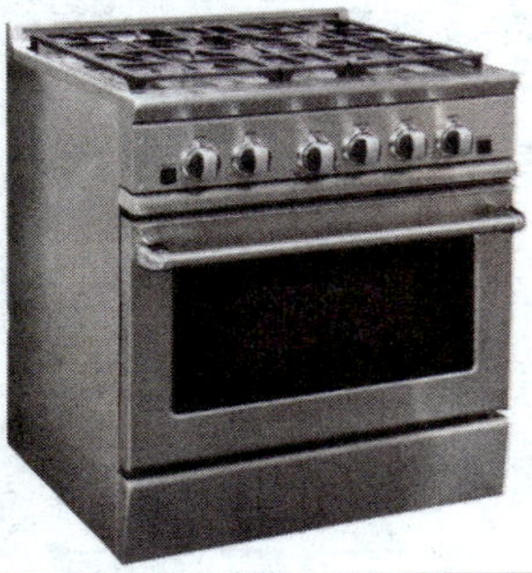

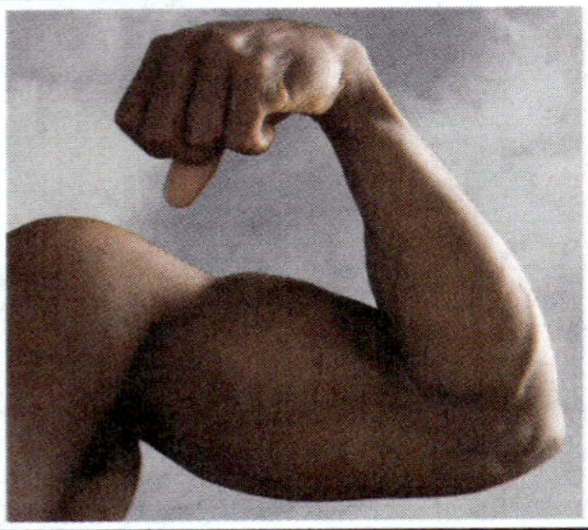

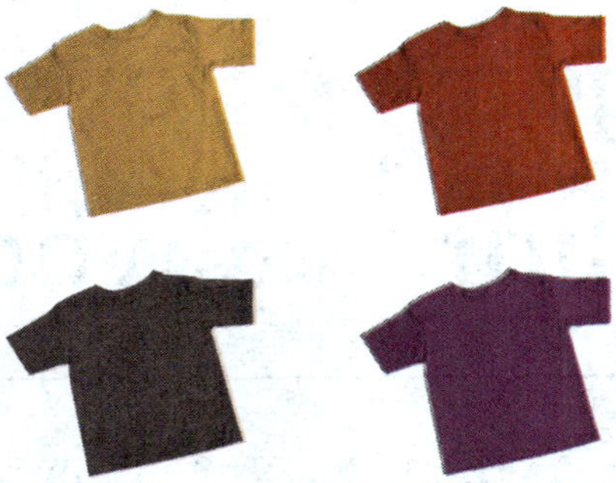

mother stove shirt cop arm
fish stoves shirts cops

My name is _____.

133

1. Who slid in the mud?
   - a cow
   - a mole
   - a snake
   - a goat
   - a pig
   - Bob

2. The goat and the pig sat on ▇▇▇.
   - a tree
   - a rug
   - a rock
   - grass

3. What did the rug run into?
   - a tree
   - a rug
   - a rock
   - grass

4. Who said, "We can slide some more."?
   - a snake
   - the pig
   - the goat
   - Bob

barn
burn
fire
free
hot
flames

stoves
stores
stones
rocks
ropes
rings

cold
rain
soaked
hot
dark
snow

trails
road
roads
part
parts
paths

Side 1

barking   ship   running   eating
digging   ships   sleeping

under   wish   first   eating
things   sneak   hurt   stay

Side 2

My name is _____.

robber

ship

cop

gold

stop

shop

I will take the _____ from her _____.

started   thing   waited   play

sneak   wish   ship   leave

1. Pam liv<u>ed</u> ▬.
   - in a home
   - on a ship
   - on a hill
   - in a tree

2. What did Pam have on h<u>er</u> ship?
   - a shop
   - a s<u>ai</u>l
   - a big lump
   - a s<u>ea</u>l

3. In h<u>er</u> shop <u>sh</u>e had ▬.
   - a big lump
   - gold
   - corn
   - goats

4. Pam hid h<u>er</u> gold so it was ▬.
   - not in a big lump
   - in a big lump
   - in a saf<u>e</u>
   - some thing you see in a shop

5. Wh<u>o</u> said, "I will sn<u>ea</u>k into that ship."?
   - Pam
   - a cop
   - a robber
   - a s<u>ea</u>l

fine	bird	lip
smil<u>e</u>	b<u>ar</u>	teeth
sore	coat	slip
h<u>ar</u>d	burn	smil<u>e</u>
h<u>ur</u>t	crow	t<u>ear</u>
cry	grow	t<u>ear</u>s

Side 2

My nam_e is _____.

I will sneak into _____
Pam's _____.

ship
robber
shop
rop_e
b<u>oa</u>t
c<u>oa</u>t

k
m
y

ships   boat   first   play   sneak
were   under   dark   while

Side 1

1. A robber had a plan to ▢.
   - take Pam's ship
   - take Pam's shop
   - sneak into Pam's hole
   - take Pam's gold
   - sneak into Pam's shop
   - sneak into Pam's cave

2. How did the robber go to Pam's ship?
   - in a car
   - in a bus
   - in a boat
   - in a ship

3. The robber said, "I will ▢."
   - sneak into Pam's shop
   - go up the side of this shop
   - sleep
   - take Pam's boat
   - go up this hill
   - go up the side of this ship

4. Did he know Pam hid her gold? _ _ _ _

5. What was it like in Pam's shop?
   - sweet
   - still
   - dark
   - dart
   - soaked

side   slide   burn   clock   clocks

Side 2

What Jan Sings

Jan liked to sing, but she made her mother sick of her singing.

Now Jan and her mother sing lots of fine things. If you are near Jan's home, you can hear that singing.

The end.

One day her mother spoke to Jan. Her mother said, "I like the way you sing, but you sing the same thing over and over. Can you sing other things?"
Jan said, "I like to sing the same thing."

Her mother said, "I will do some thing for you if you sing more than one thing. What can I do for you?"
Jan said, "Will you sing with me?"
Jan's mother said, "Yes."

My name is _____.

1. Who came to take Pam's gold?
   - a robber
   - Bob
   - Pam
   - a cop

2. What did the robber see?
   - gold
   - rocks
   - grass
   - sacks
   - clocks
   - locks
   - a lamp

3. ▢ cops grabbed the robber.
   - One
   - Two
   - Three
   - Four

4. What was made of gold?
   - a clock
   - a rock
   - a lump
   - a lamp

5. It was hard for the cop to ▢.
   - pick up the lump
   - hide the lamp
   - pick up the lamp
   - hide the lump

- kicked
- hikes
- hiding
- hated
- hearing
- hiked

- hikes
- hearing
- kicked
- hiked
- hated
- hiding

Side 1

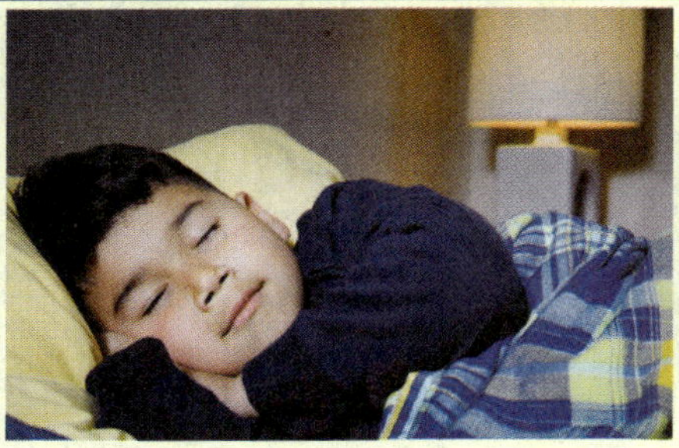

slip	tim**e**	ant
sips	tr**ai**n	ants
sleep	tr**ai**ns	bee
name	clock	bees
nap	clap	bug
nin**e**	claps	bugs

| **11** to too t**wo** tap | C see s**ea** s**ea**t | s**ai**ls s**ai**l sal**e**s sal**e** |

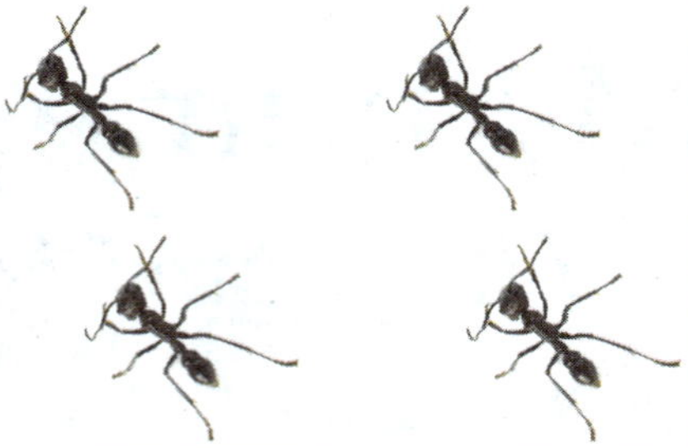

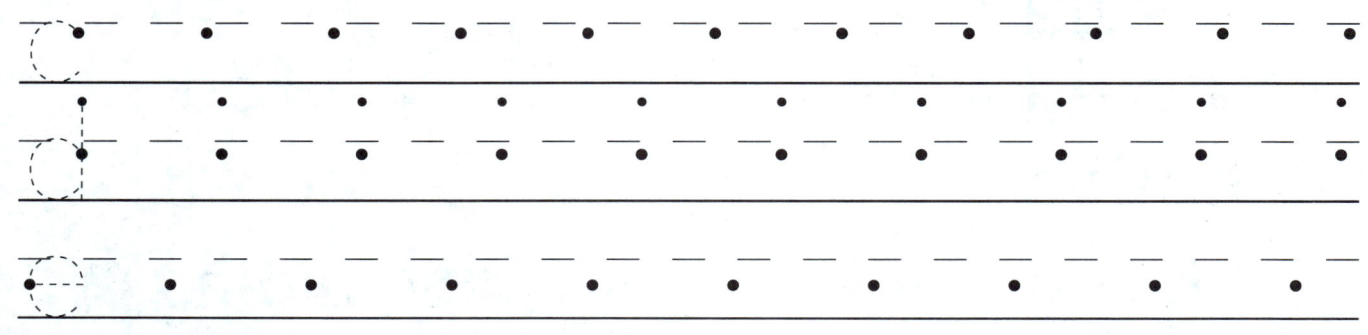

Side 2

My nam<u>e</u> is _____.

What I sing will _____ bring _____.

I don't think _____.

m<u>o</u>th<u>er</u>
ring
rain
that
so
Sid

starter   ears   teeth   barking
mother   cash   away   sailed

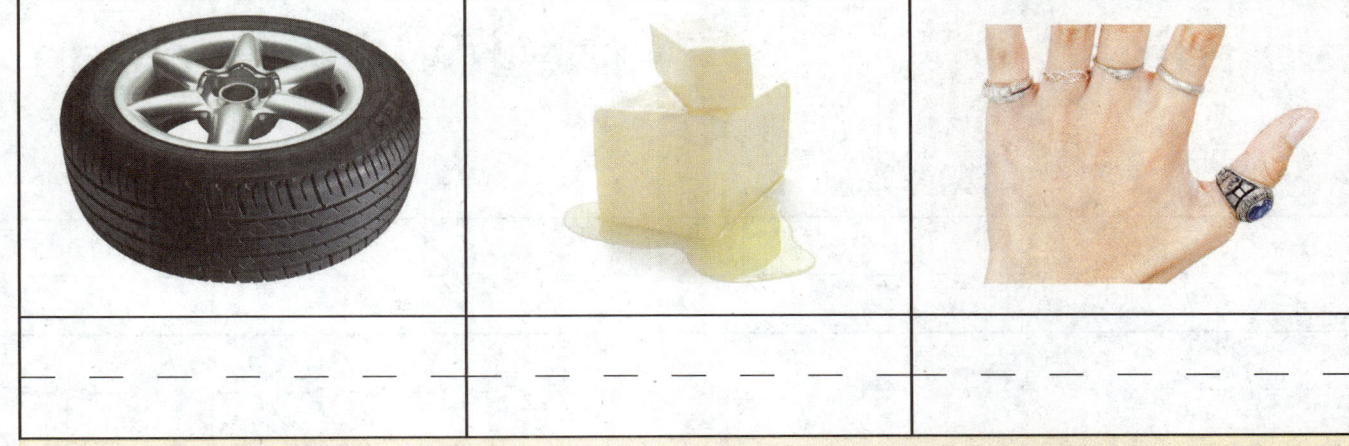

but<u>t</u><u>er</u>   ring   rings   <u>wh</u>eel   <u>wh</u>eels

Side 1

1. Sid liked things that were ▮.
   • hot   • soaked   • clean   • cold

2. The town had lots ▮.
   • of dirt   • of trees   • of grass   • of leaves

3. Sid's plan to make it rain was by ▮.
   • sleeping   • singing   • running   • eating

4. Sid's mom said, "I don't think singing will make ▮."
   • rain   • sun shine   • it dark   • a cake

5. After Sid started to sing ▮.
   • it started to snow   • it was hot
   • the sky got dark   • it made dirt
   • it rained   • the town was clean

Side 2

My nam**e** is _____.

| turtle | batter | little | bitter | fox | butter | sneak |

| showed | | turtle | | batter | | eating |
| later | | that | | start | | wish |

| napped | hiker | throw | stir | ants |

Side 1

1. The little turtle asked her mom to ▮.
   • go to the farm   • bake a cake   • eat cake   • meet a fox

2. What did the mom need for the cake?
   • sweet bitter   • sweet butter
   • bitter butter   • bitter batter

3. The mom gave the little turtle some ▮.
   • cash   • cake   • cans   • butter

4. Who stopped the little turtle near the farm?
   • the mom   • the farmer   • a cow   • a fox

5. The fox ▮.
   • stopped the mom   • sold bitter butter
   • stopped the little turtle
   • said he had sweet butter   • sold sweet butter
   • was going to throw bitter butter away

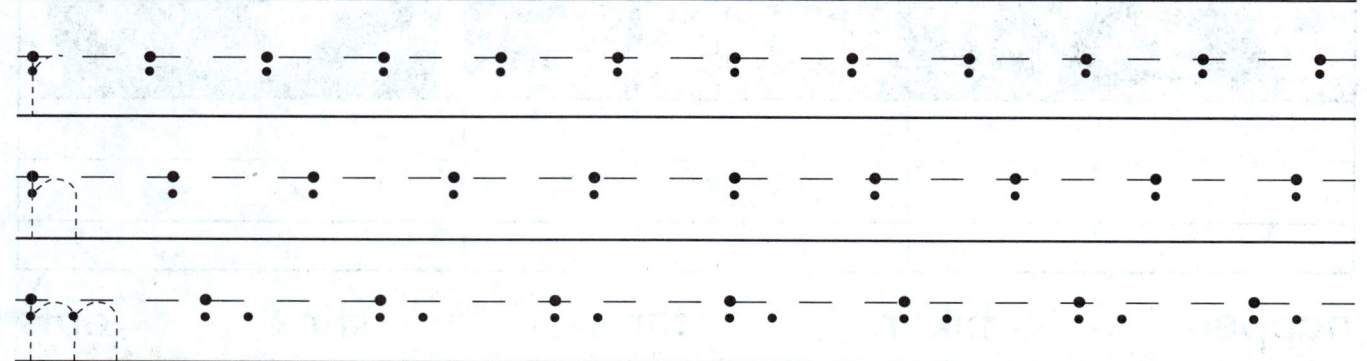

Side 2

My name is _____.

Can I _____ that cak**e**?

li**tt**le
cak**e**
hat**e**
tast**e**
t**ur**tle
mom
eat

h**ar**d
si**ng**s
hand
hands
ring
rings

stov**e**
stov**e**s
stick
rop**e**
hot
flam**e**

from
foam
fo**u**r
for

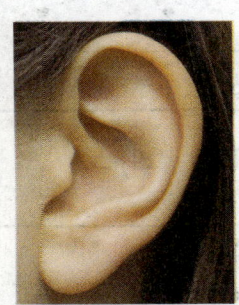

her
h**ea**r
her**e**
h**ur**t

Side 1

1. The ▨ fox sold butter to the little turtle.
   • black   • red   • brown   • wise

2. That butter was ▨.
   • sweet   • bitter   • little   • old

3. Who made cake batter?
   • the fox   • Bob
   • the little turtle   • the mother turtle

4. The turtles ▨ while the cake baked.
   • napped   • played   • waited   • ate

5. What did the little turtle say as she ate the cake?
   • yuck   • yum   • not bad   • yes

| white | cash | soap | play | start |
| trails | thinking | waited | | robber |

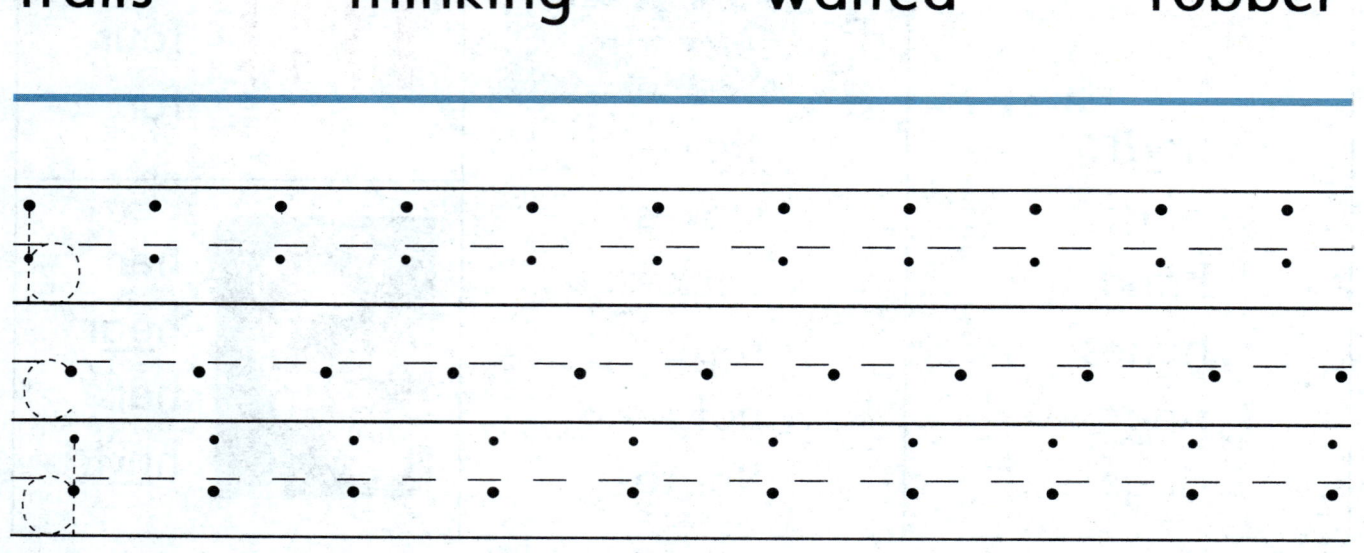

Side 2

TEST 14
140

My name is _____.

1. _____ 2. _____

3. _____ 4. _____

 ur   x   ir

But Sid started to sing. In a little while, rain came down.

Sid's mom said, "I do not know what to think."

Sid smiled and said, "I think the town is clean."

And it was.

The end.

Sid Cleans Up the Town

Sid liked things that were clean. But the town he lived in had lots of dirt.

Side 1

TEST 14

Sid liked things that were clean. But the town he lived in had lots of dirt.
 Sid told his mom, "I will make it rain. The rain will make this town clean."
 His mom asked, "How will you do that?"

---

1. brown
2. grabbed
3. fox
4. luck

1. bitter
2. shirt
3. bird
4. turtle

1. bake
2. hiding
3. leaving
4. sweet

What I sing will bring rain.

I don't think so.

Sid told his mom, "I will make this town clean."
 His mom asked, "How will you do that?
 Sid said, "I will make it rain. The rain will clean the dirt away.

"But how will you make it rain?"
 Sid said, "I will sing. What I sing will bring rain."
 His mom said, "I don't think singing will make rain."

Side 2

My name is _____.

Who sold you this butter?

The _____ _____.

| bitter | brown | turtle | batter | fox |
| little | cake | butter | mother | town |

Side 1

1. What did the turtles think of the cake?
   - It was fine.
   - Bitter butter made it bitter.
   - Sweet butter made it fine.
   - It was bitter.
   - Yum.
   - Yuck.

2. Who tasted the cake first?
   - mom
   - fox
   - little turtle
   - farmer

3. Who tasted the cake next?
   - mom
   - fox
   - little turtle
   - farmer

4. Who did the turtles plan to see?
   - mom
   - fox
   - little turtle
   - farmer

hill   hills   seat   seats   arm   arms

turn   path   cash   hard
really   ears   things trains

Side 2

My name is _____.

1. The turtles visited ▇▇▇▇.
   - the fox
   - the barn
   - Bob
   - the big one

2. What did the turtles bring the fox?
   - sweet butter
   - bitter butter
   - cash
   - a cake

3. Was that cake sweet? _____

4. How did that cake taste?
   - bitter
   - sweet
   - fine
   - like grass

5. The fox said "▇▇▇▇"
   - Yuck.
   - I hate cake.
   - I can do that.
   - How can I do that?
   - Show us.
   - I like it.

6. How was the fox going to eat cake?
   - slow
   - fast
   - in one day
   - in three days

Side 1

		rop**e**
		r**oa**d
		r**oa**ds
		rod**e**
kit**e**	**ear**	
kit**e**s	**ear**s	see
land	teeth	s**ea**
cat	hand	C
fins	smil**e**	seed
fly	smil**e**s	

over　　　　**stayed**　　　　**dirty**

　　chase　　　　**cards**　　　　**shame**

trails　　　　**throw**　　　　**away**

store　　cash　　box　　soaked　　pond　　ponds

My name is _____.

I need to _____ to make this _____ taste go away.

div**e**   fox   drink   turtles   batter   pond   bitter

 • A turtle sat in the sun.

 • Tw͜o goats at**e** grass.

• Tw͜o bugs were with a turtle.

• Tw͜o goats see three bugs.

 • A turtle mixed batter.

1. The fox ate the cake ____.
   • over and over   • slow   • in three days   • fast

2. The cake tasted ____.
   • fine   • like grass   • bitter   • sweet

3. After the fox ate the cake, he said, "I need something ____."
   • to drink   • to eat   • to see   • to read

4. What did the fox do?
   • ran to the farm   • ran to the pond
   • dove in the pond   • sat next to the pond
   • drink and drink   • dove and dove

   _____
   _ _ _ _

5. Did the cake leave a bad taste? _____

6. The fox sold bitter butter ____ time after that.
   • no   • one   • two   • three

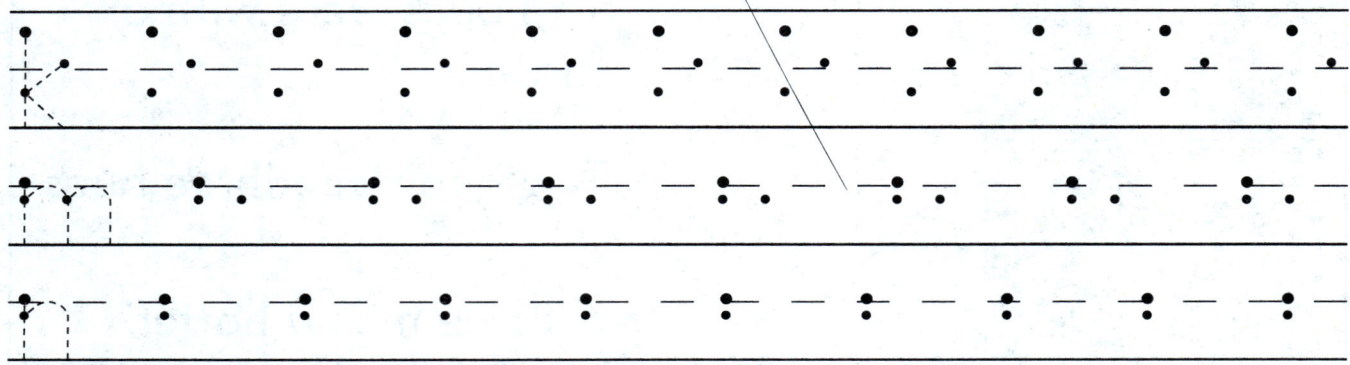

Side 2

My name is ____________.

1. Fish swim in ____.
   - drinking cups
   - rivers
   - sees
   - seas
   - ponds
   - likes
   - lakes

2. Which of these things that swim are not fish?
   - whales
   - whale sharks
   - seals
   - goldfish
   - sharks
   - turtles

3. Which of these things that swim are fish?
   - whales
   - whale sharks
   - seals
   - goldfish
   - sharks
   - turtles

4. No other fish grows to be as big as a ____.
   - whale
   - goldfish
   - seal
   - whale shark

5. A whale shark can grow to be ____ feet from end to end.
   - 6
   - 4
   - 14
   - 40

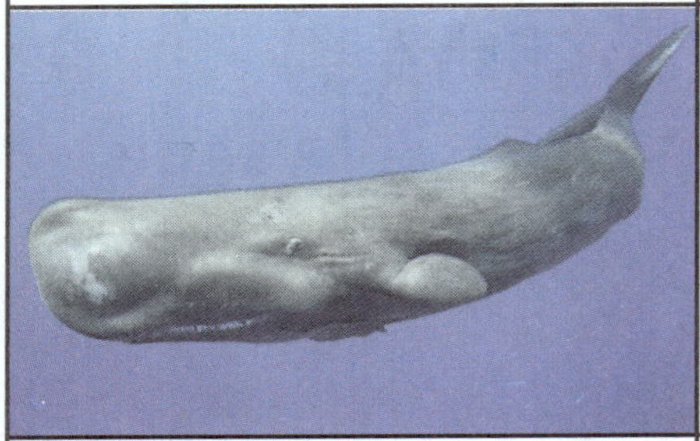

goldfish   whal**e**   turtle   s**ea**l   sh**a**rk
whal**e**s   whal**e**   turtles   s**ea**ls   sh**a**rks

A fox dov**e** in a pond.

A goat sat in the back s**ea**t.

A fox was n**e**xt to a p**ai**l.

A pig can driv**e** a c**ar**.

A fox wor**e** a hat.

A baby fox st**a**rted to cry.

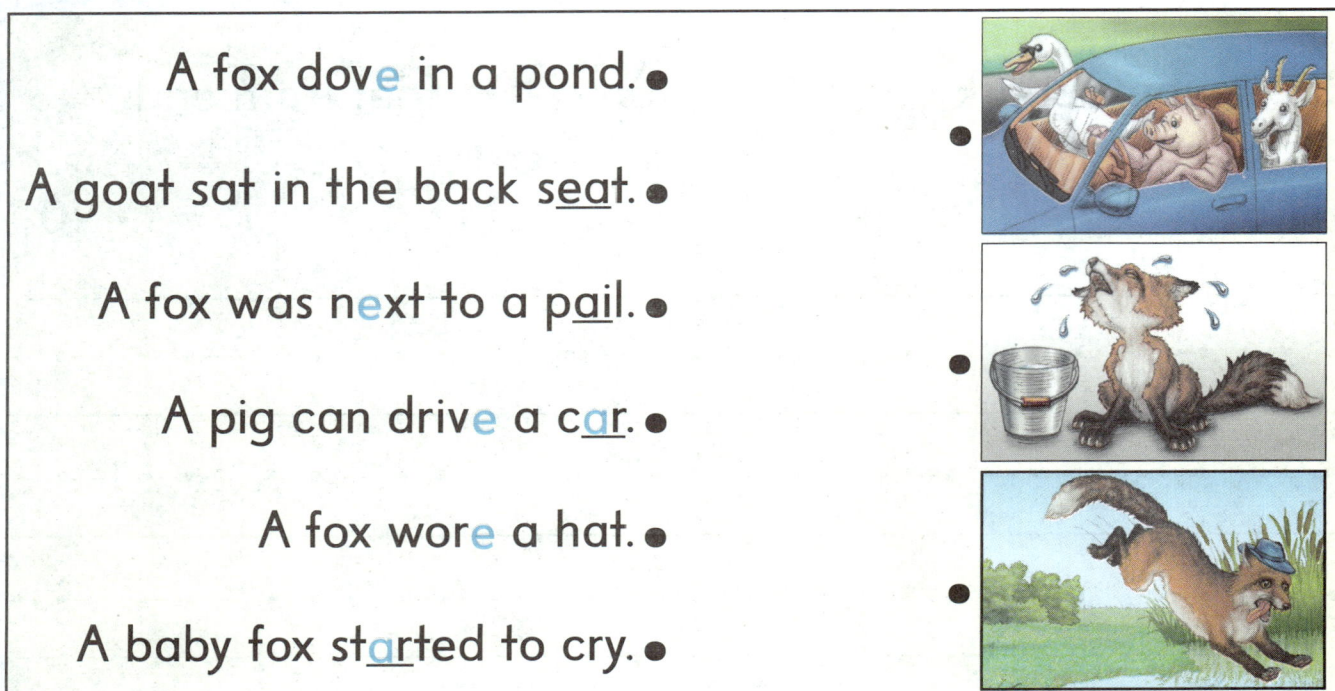

Side 2

My name is _____.

other   sister   Jill   first   turn   brother   burn

1. Who was Jill?
   - a bug
   - a rat
   - a mole
   - a leaf

2. Why did Jill's brother and sister not like playing with Jill?
   - She spoke like the big one.
   - She wins.
   - She swims.
   - She bit.

3. After Jill bit her brother, he and his sister
   - played some more.
   - bit Jill.
   - ran home.
   - told her, "We don't like playing with a bug who bites."
   - told her, "Go home."
   - told her, "It's Jill's turn."

Side 1

| cold | hiding | digging | rivers | flames |

1. What swims in rivers, seas, ponds, and lakes?
   • fish • roads • paths • cars
   • some things that are not fish • trains

2. Which of these things are fish?
   • whale sharks • whales • sharks
   • turtles • seals • goldfish

3. Which of these things are not fish?
   • whale sharks • whales • sharks
   • turtles • seals • goldfish

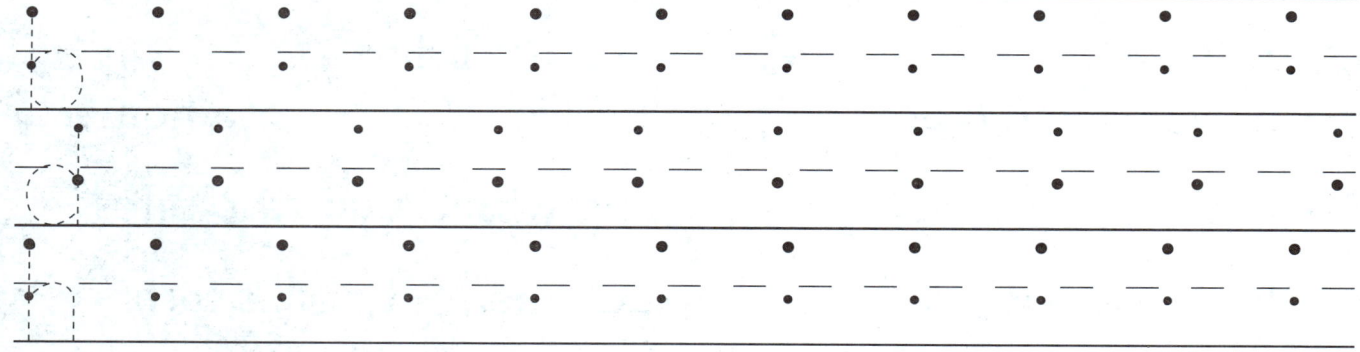

How Pam Hid Her Gold

Pam had a shop on her ship. One thing in that shop was lots of gold.

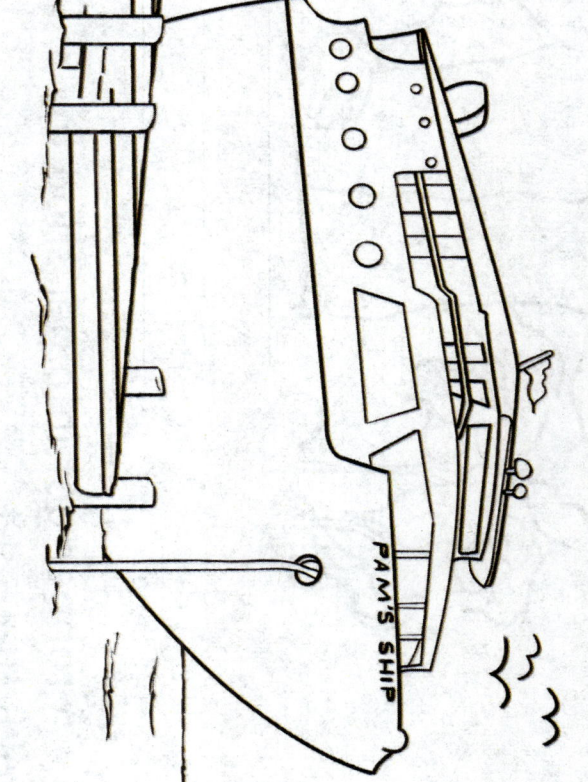

One cop grabbed the lamp. He said, "I can't pick up this lamp."

The other cop said, "I know why you can't pick it up. It's made of gold. Ho, ho, ho."

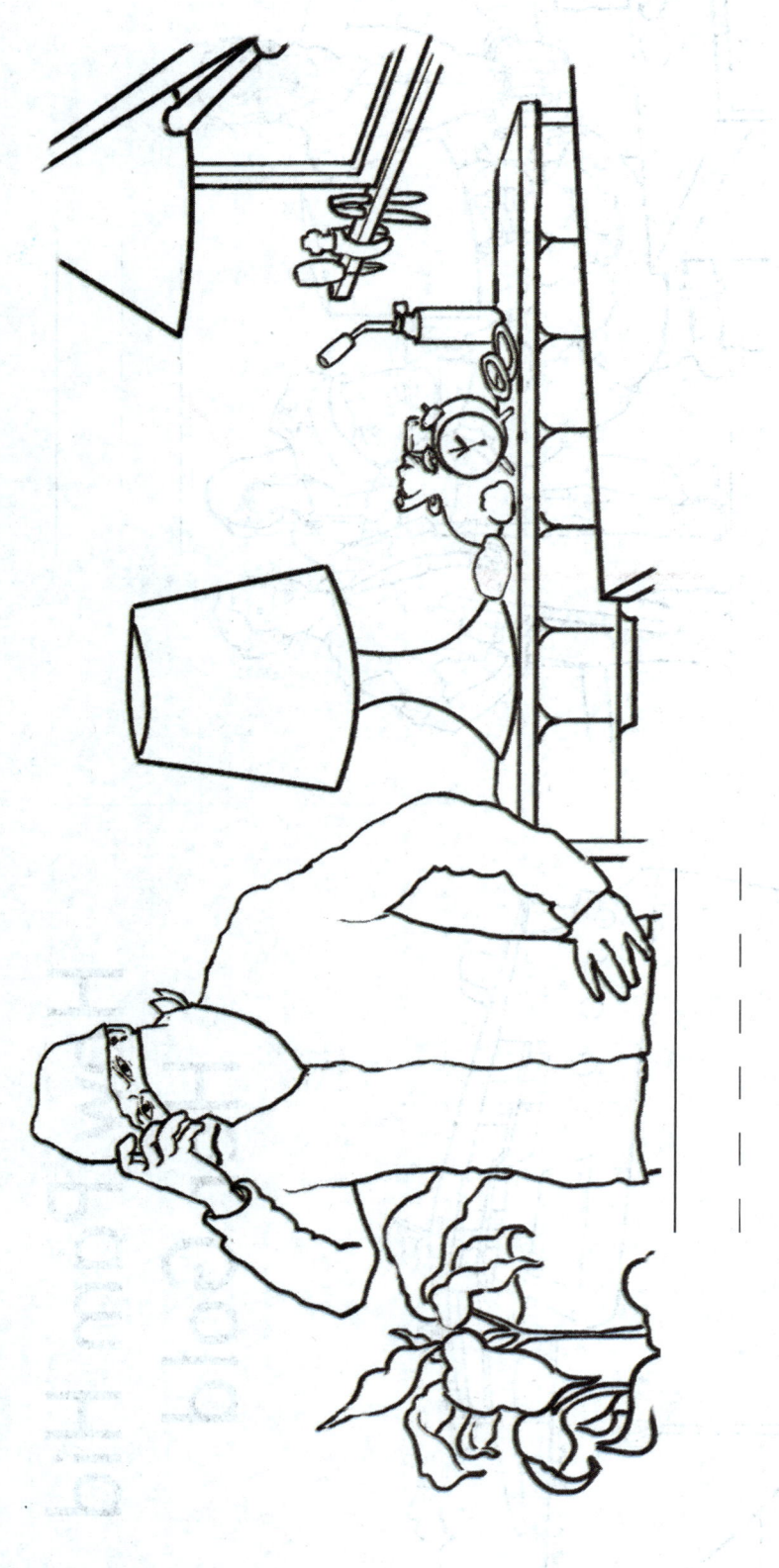

A robber got into her shop to take the gold.
He said, "I see sacks and rocks and clocks. And I see a big lamp. But I see no gold."

At last, he gave up. Just as he was leaving, two cops came and grabbed him.
 Later, the cops asked Pam, "Can you show us how you hide the gold?" She said, "If you pick up the big lamp, you will know how I hide the gold."

My name is _____.

I will dive _____.

after
Jill
tiny
you
bug
No
big
with

1. The bugs w<u>ere</u> going to ▨.
   • driv**e**   • eat   • div**e** from a tree
   • swim   • div**e** into a pond   • nap

2. The bugs came to a ▨.
   • bag   • baby   • tiny bug   • baby bug

3. The little bug said, "I will ▨."
   • div**e** with you   • bit**e** you   • sleep   • driv**e** you

4. Jill told the little bug, "▨."
   • Yes   • No   • S<u>t</u><u>ay</u> here   • Leave this tree
   • I will bit**e** you   • I will kiss you

Side 1

Her name is on a ship.

Will he be late?

He drank and drank.

She dug a hole.

He did not stay near the path.

She had a gold lamp.

He sold bitter butter.

She made a hole in a snake's home.

really   trails   things   teeth

brother   reach   sharks   which

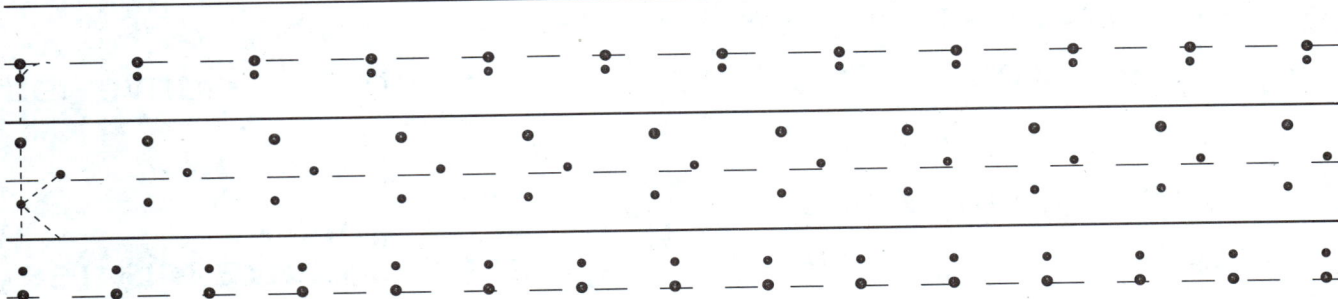

Side 2

147

My name is _____.

That little bug can really _____.

| sing |
| Chomp |
| Jill |
| bag |
| bite |
| bug |
| tiny |
| bit |

"Oh. That h<u>ur</u>ts."

"I see a big lamp."

"We hate bitter butter."

"I'm going to run home."

"You have to <u>sho</u>w us you like it."

"I will take her gold."

Side 1

1. The little bugs said, "_____."
   - That is fine
   - That is mean
   - I don't bite other bugs
   - I bite other bugs
   - I can bite really hot
   - I can bite really hard

2. Jill bit _____.
   - a man
   - the tiny bug
   - a big leaf
   - a stick

3. Did Jill bite the stick so it broke? _____

4. The little bug _____.
   - broke a stick
   - made a mark on a stick
   - broke three more sticks
   - broke another stick
   - made marks on two more sticks

going ___   think ___   into ___   started ___

sharks ___   jumped ___   spring ___

summer ___   only ___   bites ___

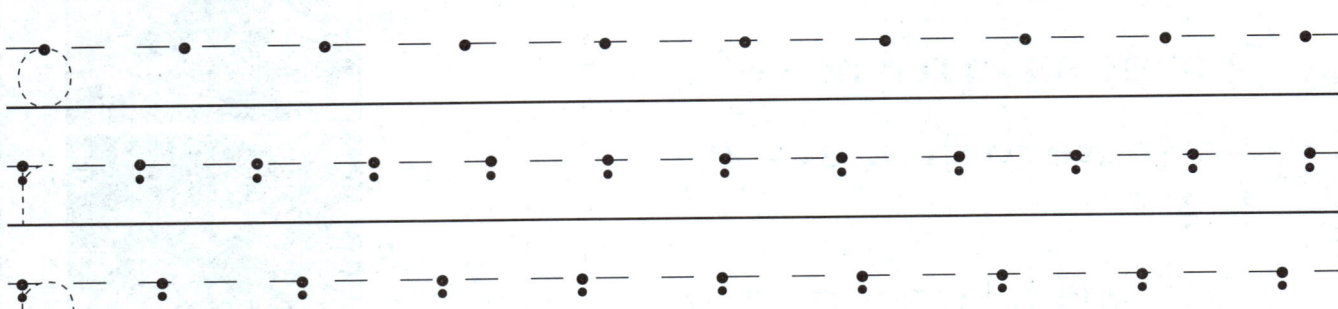

Side 2

My name is _____.

148

Later, we can go _____ _____ .

and
tiny
Jill
brother
hiking
sister
sun
sky

broke ____   body ____   river ____   shorts ____

under ____   leaves ____   story ____   storm ____

Side 1

1. Who broke two sticks with his bite?
   • Jill   • the little bug   • Jill's sister   • Jill's brother

2. The little bug ▓▓▓ other bugs.
   • will try to bite   • will try not to bite
   • will bite   • will eat

3. After the little bug bit two sticks, Jill said "▓▓▓."
   • I was jumping   • I don't bite other bugs
   • I was just kidding   • I do bite other bugs
   • That is a fine thing to do
   • That is a mean thing to do

4. Those four bugs ▓▓▓.
   • became pals   • hated each other
   • bit each other   • hiked with each other
   • dove with each other   • kicked each other

5. Who said, "Jill, do you mean that?"
   • Jill   • Jill's brother   • the little bug   • Jill's sister

6. Jill bit other bugs ▓▓▓ times after that day.
   • five   • four   • three   • no

Side 2

149

My nam**e** is _____.

Row, row, _____
_____
the _____.

Rain, _____,
clean _____
_____.

| rain | town | down | Sid | boat |
| Jan | row | this | his |

Side 1

1. Sid was singing to ▇▇▇.
   - have fun
   - make it rain
   - make his mom sick
   - clean the town
   - sing with his mom

2. Jan was singing ▇▇▇.
   - Row, row, row the boat
   - Rain, rain go away
   - Rain, rain clean this town
   - things one time
   - things two times
   - things over and over

3. Who sings with each other?
   - Sid
   - Jan
   - Jan's mom
   - Sid's mom
   - Jill
   - the little bug

grass	sky	seal
grasses	sun	seals
leaf	rain	fish
leaves	ran	shark
tree	store	sharks
trees	storm	whale shark

Side 2

My name is _____.

1. _____   2. _____

3. _____   4. _____

 ___ or   ch ___ ol

The big turtle said, "I had a sun bath. Now I will have a rain bath. Ho ho."

Two brown turtles lived in the weeds near a pond. One day the turtles were sitting on some rocks. The big turtle said, "I really like this sun."

Side 1

The mum turtle began to make the batter. She said, "We mix sweet butter into the batter."

But she had bitter butter. And bitter butter won't make a sweet cake.

After the batter was made, the turtles waited while the cake baked.

---

1. drink
2. <u>ch</u>omp
3. sh<u>or</u>t
4. t<u>ur</u>n

1. <u>visit</u>ed
2. <u>some</u>body
3. <u>becam</u>e
4. <u>think</u>ing

1. only
2. bit<u>ing</u>
3. r<u>ea</u>lly
4. brother

In a while, the sky became dark. The little turtle said, "I think it will start to rain. We need to go home."

But the big turtle said, "No. I will stay here. The sun will come back."

The sun did not come back. Rain came down.

My name is _____.

1. Jan's mom showed her how to make ▓▓▓.
   - mud cakes
   - soap cars
   - road turtles
   - rock turtles
   - pants
   - shirts

2. Jan made those things ▓▓▓.
   - under and under
   - over and over
   - one time
   - two times

3. Jan said that she will take the turtles to ▓▓▓.
   - grass
   - store
   - a beach
   - a hill

4. What did Jan make next?
   - shirts
   - boats
   - bikes
   - cars

---

birds ____   open ____   female ____   sticks ____

buses ____   shirts ____   apple ____   rolling ____

---

beach   short   shark   brother

gold   story   dirty   burns

clean   really   thank   hard

Side 1

She made lots of shirts.

His singing made rain.

It swims in seas but is not a fish.

He made the town clean.

Stone turtles were on her rug.

She dug to free feet.

My name is _____.

1. Jan said, "I will make a shirt for somebody who is ▇▇▇▇."

   - shorter than I am
   - older than I am
   - faster than I am
   - bigger than I am

2. Did she make a shirt that was bigger than the others?

   _ _ _ _

3. Jan's mom said, "▇▇▇▇▇."

   - Six moms can eat it
   - Six moms can fit in it
   - I don't know
   - I think I know
   - I will show you
   - I won't show you

4. The shirt ▇▇▇▇▇.

   - keeps dirt on a car
   - keeps a car clean
   - is on a car
   - is under a car
   - is a bad fit
   - is a fine fit

Side 1

"No robber can find my gold." •

"I like to sing the same thing." •

"Can you make a shirt that is not the same?" •

"I know how to make this dirt go away." •

reach _____   trainer _____   mother _____   short _____

shark _____   shirt _____   goldfish _____   cheap _____

Side 2

My name is _____.   153

1. This is a story of ▇▇▇.
   - ten fish
   - ten men
   - nine men
   - six whales

2. When one man did something, ▇▇▇ more men did it too.
   - five
   - six
   - nine
   - ten

3. One day the men said, "We will go ▇▇▇."
   - fishing
   - running
   - boating
   - hiking

4. The ten men went ▇▇▇.
   - in a car
   - on bikes
   - in a van
   - on a rug
   - in a boat
   - in a lake

5. The boat they rented was made for ▇▇▇ men.
   - one
   - three
   - nine
   - ten

6. Did the boat hold those ten men? _____

7. So the men went ▇▇▇.
   - swimming
   - fishing
   - boating
   - driving

---

open ___   shore ___   became ___

riding ___   trades ___   batter ___

Side 1

bird	female	clock
birds	shore	clocks
tent	card	
tents	cards	

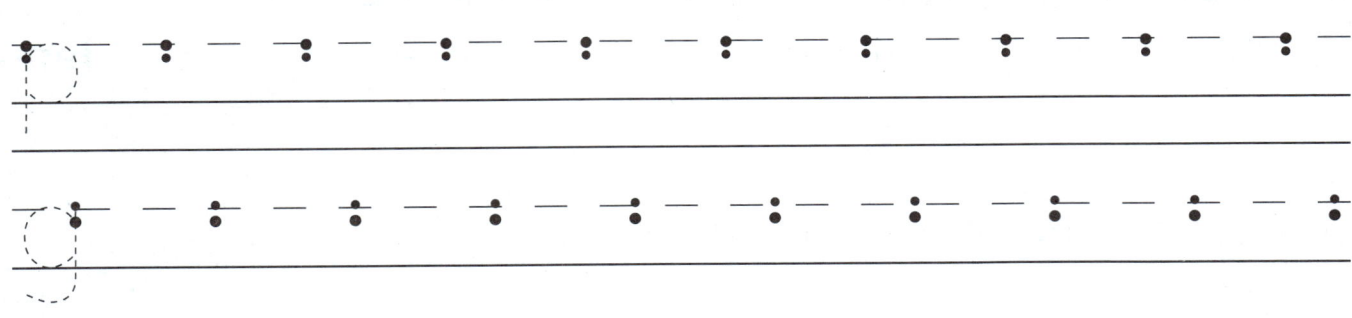

stick
sticks
bone
bones

boat
dock
ship
shore

Side 2

154

My name is _____.

... I end up with _____ than I had _____.

| corn | before | bike | became | bag |
| more | clock | Debby | sleeping | bigger |

Side 1

1. Debby was a fine ▬▬.
   - sleeper
   - trader
   - runner
   - swimmer

2. After a lot of trades, Debby had ▬▬.
   - a car
   - her first bike back
   - her first barn back
   - a store

3. She made a trade for corn that was ▬▬.
   - black
   - red
   - gold
   - white
   - old
   - not gold

4. What did Debby do with that corn?
   - burn it
   - trade some of it
   - eat some of it
   - soak some of it
   - throw some of it away
   - plant some of it

rock
rocks
stoves
stone
stones
store

green
plants
plan
grass
tree
trees

Side 2

My name is _____.

155

try

store

seal

stove

sell

trade

bus

buses

baby

fox

bird

birds

Side 1

1. When Debby traded, she got ▅▅▅.
   - more things
   - two things
   - one thing
   - no things

2. After she was done trading corn ▅▅▅
   - her home was clean.
   - she had piles on rugs.
   - her mom said, "Keep these things."
   - her mom said, "Sell them."
   - her home was a mess.
   - she had piles on her bed.

3. Her mom told Debby to ▅▅▅.
   - trade
   - get more things
   - sell her things
   - throw her things away

4. After the sale, Debby had lots of ▅▅▅.
   - things
   - corn
   - cash
   - piles

5. What did Debby open?
   - stove
   - barn
   - can
   - store

hurry ___   year ___   shores ___   before ___

rolling ___   hotter ___   white ___   boating ___

Side 2

Ten Men

Ten men liked to do things with each other. When one man went to a show, the other nine men went with him. When one man went to the store, the other nine men went with him.

One day, a man said, "Let's go fishing."

The other nine men said, "Yes, let's go fishing."

So ten men got in a van, and away they went to the lake.

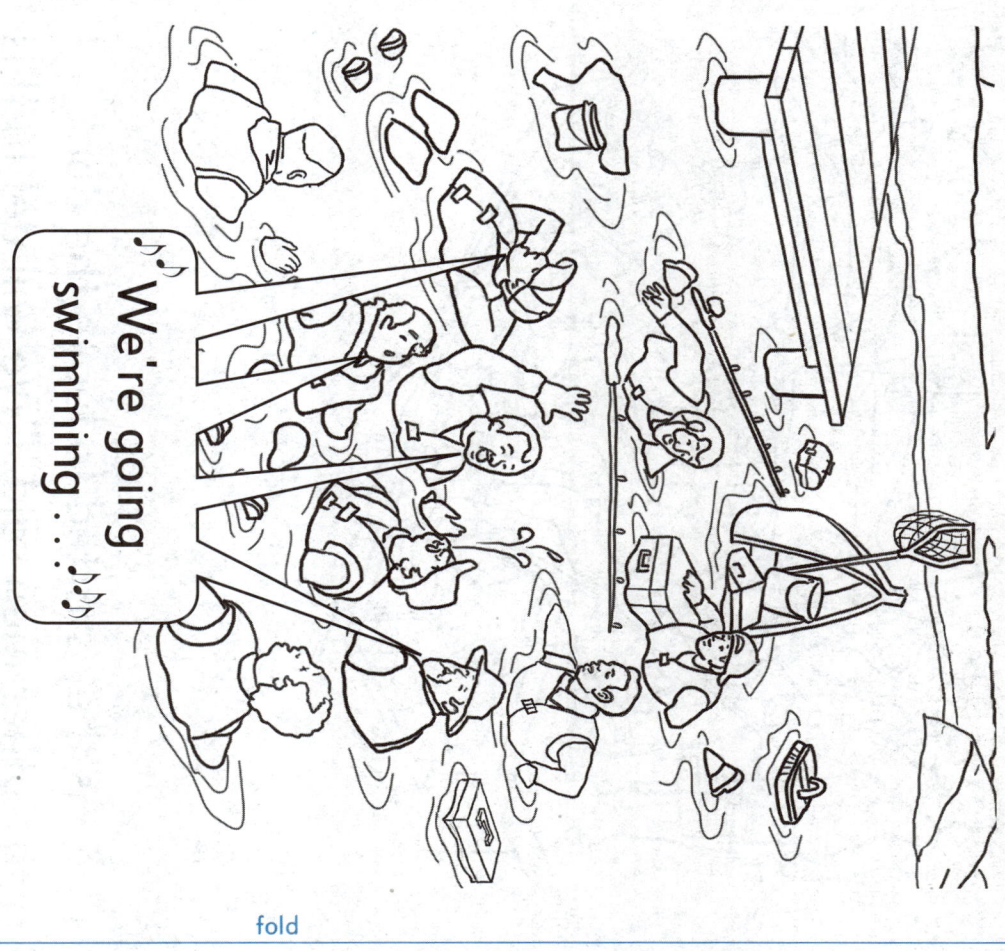

"We're going fishing..."

"We're going swimming..."

So the ten men did not go boating and did not go fishing. Those men went swimming.

The end.

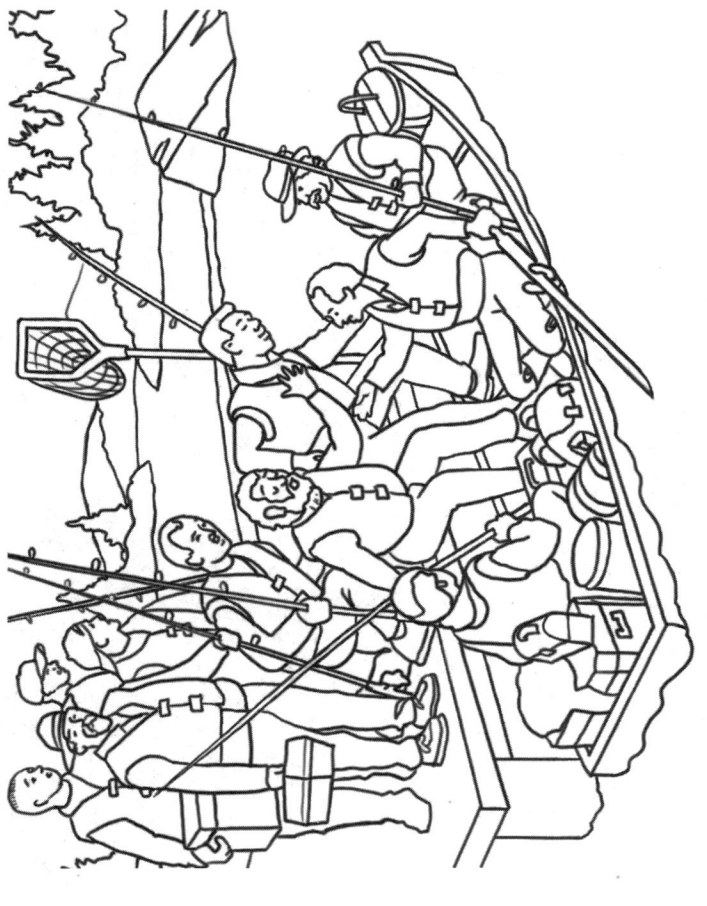

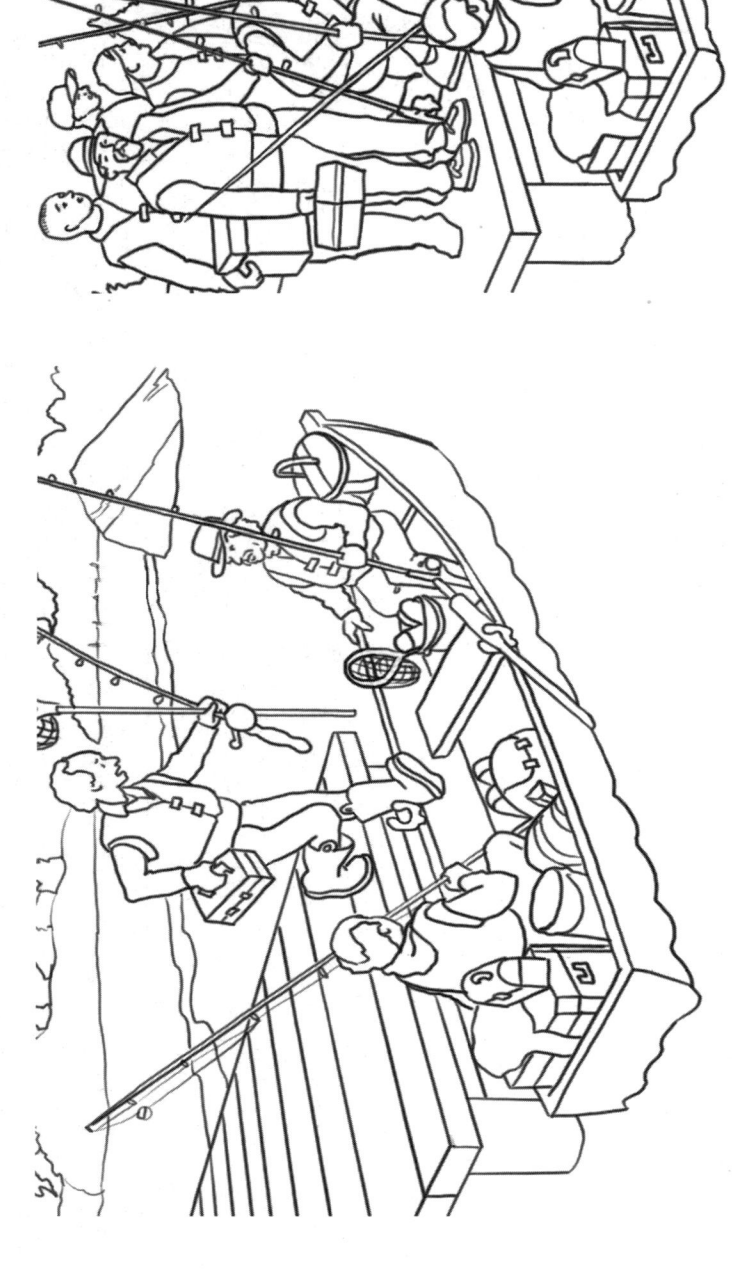

When they got to the lake, the men said, "We will rent a boat." And they did.

Only one boat was left, and it was not a big boat. It was made for three men, not ten men.

The first three men said, "We will get in this boat." And they did.

As they started to leave the dock, the other men said, "We will get in this boat, too." And they did.

Did the boat hold the men? No.

My name is _____. 156

try
swim
leg
legs
fly
wing
wings
b<u>ea</u>k
b<u>ea</u>ks
rings
filled

Birds that can fly have bones _____ with <u>air</u>.

---

1. Birds have ▇▇▇▇.
   • 2 legs   • lots of legs   • 2 wings   • 2 b<u>ea</u>ks
   • lots of f<u>ea</u>thers   • 2 f<u>ea</u>thers   • 1 wing   • 1 b<u>ea</u>k

2. When the <u>air</u> is cold, the h<u>ea</u>t of a bird's body ▇▇▇▇.
   • goes up   • stays the same   • goes down

Side 1

3. Birds that can fly have bones filled with ▬.
   - stone
   - more than air
   - air
   - feathers

4. Which birds show off to find a mate?
   - males
   - females
   - baby birds
   - big birds

5. What do male birds do to show off?
   - sing
   - make nest
   - flap wings
   - flap shirts
   - swim
   - shake tail feathers

6. Birds find a mate in the ▬.
   - snow
   - winter
   - spring
   - summer

7. After a female picks a mate ▬.
   - they live with each other
   - they make a nest
   - they leave each other
   - they eat dirt
   - the male lays eggs
   - the female lays eggs

8. Each egg has ▬ baby bird(s).
   - ten
   - six
   - three
   - one

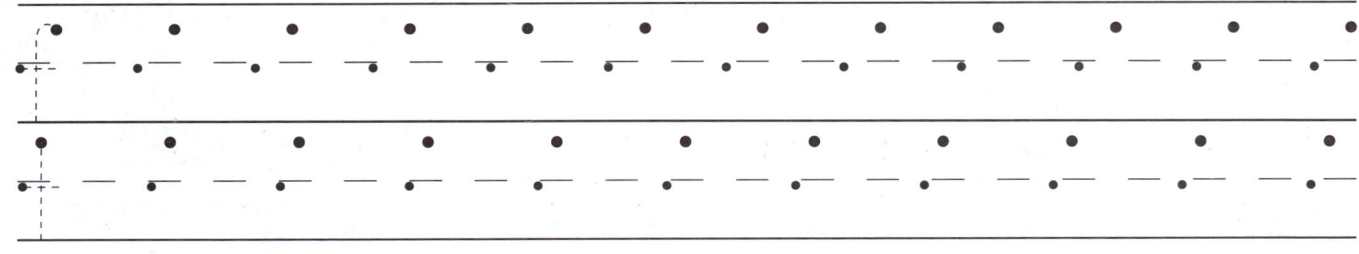

Side 2

My name is _____.

mal**e**
mal**e**s
femal**e**
femal**e**s
egg
eggs
baby
nest
nests

Only one _____ bird is in **e**ach _____.

		f**ea**ther
_____	_____	f**ea**thers
		men
		picture
		pictures
_____	_____	f**a**rmer
		f**a**rmers

Side 1

1. What do birds do before the female lays eggs?
   - lay eggs
   - fly
   - make a nest
   - swim

2. Some birds make their nests in ▓▓▓.
   - trees that have died
   - mud holes
   - trees that have not died
   - grass
   - flames
   - homes like your home

3. Mother birds can lay up to ▓▓▓ eggs.
   - 3
   - 6
   - 10
   - 100
   - 32
   - 9

4. Birds sit on eggs so they won't get ▓▓▓.
   - cold
   - wet
   - hot
   - dry

5. The baby bird inside the egg will ▓▓▓ if it gets cold.
   - fly
   - live
   - eat
   - die

6. Male and female birds ▓▓▓.
   - take turns sitting on leaves
   - take turns sitting on the eggs
   - leave the eggs for a week
   - hunt if they are not sitting on the eggs
   - swim if they are not sitting on the eggs
   - find other mates

Side 2

My name is _____.   158

1. The female bird hunts for things to eat when she is not sitting on the nest.   Birds   Bird Nests

2. Each bird has a beak.   Birds   Bird Nests

3. One thing male birds do is show off to female birds.   Birds   Bird Nests

4. Some birds make their nests in trees that died.   Birds   Bird Nests

5. Baby birds inside eggs will die if they get too cold.   Birds   Bird Nests

6. Birds that can fly have bones filled with air.   Birds   Bird Nests

7. The male bird and female bird take turns sitting on their eggs.   Birds   Bird Nests

8. The heat of the bird's body stays the same.   Birds   Bird Nests

Side 1

1. Which seeds can we eat?
   - rocks
   - beans
   - stones
   - cobs
   - beaks
   - corn

2. Where do beans grow?
   - on cobs
   - in homes
   - in pods
   - on sticks

3. We ▆▆▆ a lot of beans before we eat them.
   - drink
   - hide
   - throw away
   - cook

4. Where do corn kernels grow?
   - on cobs
   - in homes
   - in pods
   - on sticks

5. What kind of corn pops when it gets hot?
   - popcar
   - popcorn
   - popcart
   - hotcorn

read
red
brown
green

brown
grass
greet
green

animal
apples
apple
a pile

Side 2

cave	bird	cats
wave	bug	cat
lake	bugs	kittens
like	wings	kitten
beach	fly	animals
shore	arms	feathers

| feather | female | diving | throw | hole |
| feathers | females | beach | | holes |

Side 3

A cold wind made him shak**e**.

She had shorts on.

They went to sleep.

He had shorts on.

He was under a cat.

He ran on a tr<u>ai</u>l in the park.

He had a coat on.

She went hik<u>ing</u> on the hill.

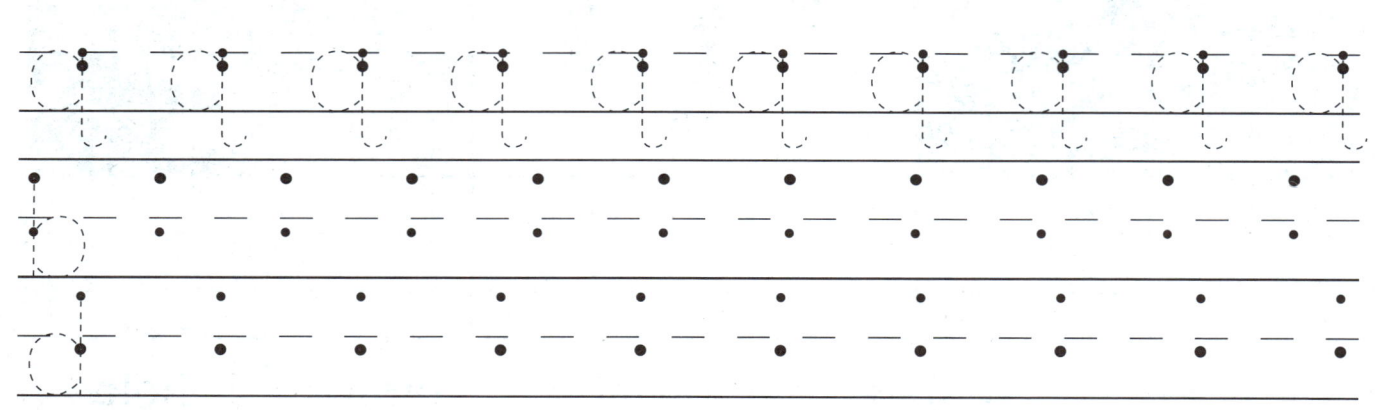

My name is _____.

1. Rice grows in really wet dirt.   Seeds   Grass Seeds

2. We grind up wheat seeds to make a powder.   Seeds   Grass Seeds

3. This seed pops when it gets hot.   Seeds   Grass Seeds

4. Batter is made of wheat, eggs, milk, and butter.   Seeds   Grass Seeds

5. Beans grow in pods.   Seeds   Grass Seeds

6. Wheat and rice are seeds we eat.   Seeds   Grass Seeds

7. Corn kernels grow on cobs.   Seeds   Grass Seeds

Side 1

1. What part of some kinds of grass can you eat?
   - cobs
   - pods
   - seeds
   - ears

2. What kind of grass seeds do we eat?
   - corn
   - apples
   - beans
   - wheat
   - short grass
   - tiny grass
   - rice
   - sharks

3. We grind wheat seeds to make a ▉.
   - powder
   - home
   - hole
   - nest

4. Rice grows in holes that are very ▉.
   - tiny
   - little
   - clean
   - wet

5. Can wheat grow well where rice grows? _____

6. What do you do to rice before you eat it?
   - sit on it
   - cook it
   - burn it
   - grind it

Side 2

You can eat the _____ _____ of some _____.

| ear | grass | pods | bread | powder |
| of | seeds | loaf | rice | wheat | cobs |

| whale | seal | shark | goldfish | snake | turtle |
| whales | seals | sharks | | snakes | turtles |

Side 3

A turtle sat in the sun. •

Two goats ate grass. •

They went for a drive. •

A bird, a pig, and a goat went for a ride. •

Two bugs can see her make a cake. •

A mother turtle stirred batter. •

Three bugs spoke to goats in the grass. •

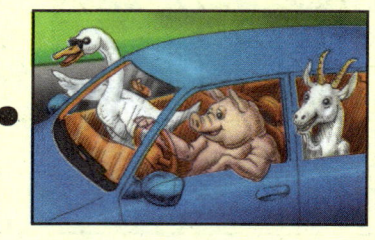

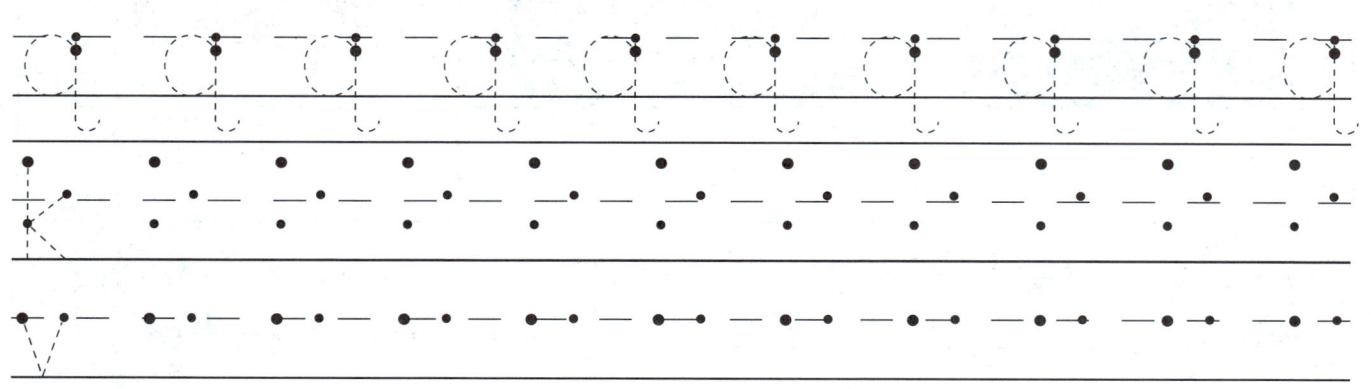

Side 4

My name is _____.

1. _____ 2. _____

3. _____ 4. _____

 z    e z

---

 Rice is another seed we eat. Rice grows in dirt that is really wet. We cook rice before we eat it.

The beans, corn, wheat and rice we eat are seeds. If we plant those seeds, we can grow bean, corn, wheat or rice plants.

Seeds We Eat

We eat seeds that grow on plants.

Beans are seeds we eat. Beans grow in pods that grow on bean plants. We cook a lot of beans before we eat them. We do not eat many kinds of bean pods.

Side 1

One class of animals is birds.
E̲ach bird has two legs, two wings, one b̲e̲a̲k, and lots of fḛa̰thers.
A lot of birds have bon̲e̲s that are filled with a̲i̲r. These birds can fly.
Birds with bon̲e̲s filled with more than a̲i̲r can't fly.
Some birds are so big that they can run with a man on them.

---

1. dock	1. h̲u̲n̲ted	1. b̲e̲f̲o̲r̲e̲	1. baby
2. whi̲c̲h̲	2. s̲h̲o̲w̲ing	2. fe̲m̲a̲l̲e̲	2. funny
3. sell	3. w̲i̲n̲ter	3. in̲s̲i̲d̲e̲	3. hurry
4. wet	4. d̲i̲v̲ing	4. p̲i̲c̲ture	4. many

We eat corn that gro̲w̲s on corn plants. A corn seed is a k̲e̲r̲nel. K̲e̲r̲nels grow̲ on corn cobs.

Corn cobs grow̲ inside green leaves. The w̲h̲o̲l̲e̲ thing is an ear of corn. We co̰o̰k some corn before we eat it. Some corn k̲e̲r̲nels pop when they get hot.

We eat some kinds of grass. We don't eat the other parts of this grass, just the seeds.

We grind up part of whe̲a̲t seeds to make a powd̲e̲r̲. We mix that powd̲e̲r̲ with eggs and milk to make things like pancakes and brḛa̰d.

PHOTO CREDITS

L111 Side 02 (ear)©Geoff du Feu/Alamy (road)Ingram Publishing (ocean)Westend61/Getty Images (dog's ears)Purestock/SuperStock (marfly)NHPA/David Chapman (beetle)©Brand X Pictures/PunchStock **L112 Side 02** (boy)McGraw-Hill Education/Eclipse Studios (smile)Ingram Publishing (boy on bike)Thinkstock Images/Getty Images (ocean)Goodshoot/Getty Images (grass)©Image Source, all rights reserved (intersection)Ryan Jones/Getty Images **L113 Side 02** (boy)F. Rombout/Pixtal/age fotostock (goat)Jessica Byrne (baby goat)Jessica Byrne (lemur tail)Profimedia/SuperStock (mouse tail)©imageBROKER/SuperStock (hive)nathanphoto/iStock/Getty Images (reading)Design Pics/Leah Warkentin (crow)Anton Harder/Getty Images (cat tail)Image Source (note)©McGraw-Hill Education **L115 Side 02** (pig)Bill Boch/Stockbyte/Getty Images (stones)Shutterstock/Herring Images (gravel)Christian Kobierski/Shutterstock (cave)Shutterstock/Zack Frank **L116 Side 02** (skating)XiXinXing/Getty Images (diving)Ingram Publishing/SuperStock (ship)Purestock/SuperStock (jumping)Andersen Ross/Blend Images LLC (dandelion)unpict/Shutterstock (train)NPS Photo, Ken Ganz (thistle)Henrik_L/iStock/Getty Images **L117 Side 02** (detective)PeopleImages.com/Digital Vision/Getty Images (dog)Mordasova Elena/Shutterstock (bike tire)©Photodisc/Getty Images (wasp nest)BanksPhotos/iStock/Getty Images (car tire)©Ingram Publishing/Alamy **L118 Side 02** (camping)PhotoObjects.net/Getty Images (sky)Marek Mnich/Getty Images (seeds)McGraw-Hill Education (car)Hannu Liivaar/Alamy **L119 Side 02** (road)Ingram Publishing (ocean)Goodshoot/Getty Images **L121 Side 02** (barn)Stockbyte/Getty Images (ship)Purestock/SuperStock (girl back)Tim Pannell/SuperStock (crying)Davi Ozolin/Moment Open/Getty Images (fire)Westend61/Getty Images (dog)Shutterstock/ESB Professional **L122 Side 02** (bees)Ralf Hettler (sky)Marek Mnich/Getty Images (lake)Shutterstock/Drepicter (money)Tetra images/Punchstock **L123 Side 02** (hive)nathanphoto/iStock/Getty Images (fish)Don Farrall/Getty Images (car)©McGraw-Hill Education (blue car)Rawpixel/iStock/Getty Images (old car)Lalocracio/iStock/Getty Images **L125 Side 01** (girl)sdominick/Getty Images (honeycomb)nayneung1/Getty Images (paths)georgeclerk/iStock/Getty Images **L125 Side 02** (dog tail)Ingram Publishing (cat tail)McGraw-Hill Education (driving)©John Lund/Blend Images LLC (stove)INSADCO Photography/Alamy (ship)Purestock/SuperStock (wheel)grafner/123RF (singing)Design Pics/Ron Nickel/Getty Images **L126 Side 02** (cat tail)McGraw-Hill Education (storefront)Stockbyte/Getty Images (sky)Marek Mnich/Getty Images (rings)Jasmin Awad/EyeEm/Getty Images (barn)©Steve Hamblin/Alamy **L127 Side 02** (singing)Design Pics/Ron Nickel/Getty Images (mom/baby)Corbis/age fotostock (farm)Shutterstock/MaxyM **L131 Side 02** (farm)Shutterstock/MaxyM (bike tire)©Photodisc/Getty Images (car tire)©Ingram Publishing/Alamy (shark)PM Images/Getty Images (wave)Purestock/SuperStock (tools)Spaces Images/Blend Images (girl)©Hero/Corbis/Glow Images **L132 Side 02** (fish)Ammit/Getty Images (stove)INSADCO Photography/Alamy (bee)Don Farrall/Getty Images (cheetah tail)Shutterstock/Valentyna Chukhlyebova (purchase)©Radius Images/Alamy Stock Photo (running)Comstock/Getty Images (police)©William Ryall 2007 (arm)©John Lund/Blend Images LLC (red shirt)Studiohio (yellow shirt)Studiohio (purple shirt)Studiohio (grey shirt)Studiohio (fox tail)Shutterstock/Ondrej Prosicky (horse tail)LOSHADENOK/iStock/Getty Images **L133 Side 01** (girl)sdominick/Getty Images (stones)Shutterstock/Herring Images (fire)Christopher Coll/iStock/Getty Images (paths)mountaintreks/Shutterstock **L133 Side 02** (ship)Purestock/SuperStock (digging)Denis Babenko/Getty Images (sleeping)Ingram Publishing/SuperStock (barking)paula sierra/Moment/Getty Images (running)BLOOM Image/Getty Images (eating)G.K. & Vikki Hart/Getty Images **L134 Side 02** (crow)Anton Harder/Getty Images (smile)Ingram Publishing (boy)photodeti © 123RF.com **L135 Side 02** (candle)©SuperStock/age fotostock (clocks)©Image Source, all rights reserved **L136 Side 02** (boy)McGraw-Hill Education/Eclipse Studios (sleeping)Blend Images/Getty Images (clock)©McGraw-Hill Education (boat)Niels-DK/Alamy (ant)©IT Stock Free/Alamy **L137 Side 01** (tire)©Ingram Publishing/Alamy (butter)©2/James Worrell/Ocean/Corbis (hand)McGraw-Hill Education **L138 Side 01** (hiking)Alpha and Omega Collection/Alamy (sleeping)Ingram Publishing (stirring)©McGraw-Hill Education **L139 Side 01** (ear)Geoff du Feu/Alamy Stock Photo (hand)McGraw-Hill Education (stove)©Adam Gault/age fotostock **L141 Side 02** (chair)McGraw-Hill Education/Janette Beckman photographer (woman)Stockbyte/Getty Images (hill)Vladimir/YAY Micro/age fotostock **L142 Side 02** (boy)McGraw-Hill Education/Eclipse Studios (smile)Ingram Publishing (boy on bike)Thinkstock Images/Getty Images (money)Tetra images/Punchstock (kite)Clicknique/Getty Images (dog)GlobalP/iStock/Getty Images (garden)Glow Images **L144 Side 02** (sea lion)AlexGoldblum/Getty Images (shark)Image Source/Getty Images (sea turtle)Kjeld Friis .dk/Getty Images (sharks)Mint Images/Mint Images RF/Getty Images (whale)James R.D. Scott/Getty Images (goldfish)Anthony Bradshaw/Getty Images **L145 Side 02** (fire)Design Pics/age fotostock (hiding)PhotoAlto/Alamy (shoveling)©Image Source, all rights reserved. **L149 Side 02** (tree)Tom Grill/Photographer's Choice/Getty Images (whale shark)Krzysztof Odziomek/Shutterstock (storm)WeatherVideoHD.TV **L151 Side 02** (whale)James R.D. Scott/Getty Images **L153 Side 02** (skeleton)©Comstock/Alamy (beach)Glow Images/Superstock (tents)schankz/Shutterstock (bird)schnuddel/E+/Getty Images (cards)omers/Shutterstock (clock)AlexLMX/iStock/Getty Images (girl)McGraw-Hill Education/Ken Cavanagh (jetty)invictus99/123RF **L154 Side 02** (desert)Ronnie Kaufman/Larry Hirshowitz/Getty Images (grass)©Image Source, all rights reserved. **L155 Side 01** (buses)©DigitalVues/Alamy (birds)BOONCHUAY PROMJIAM/Shutterstock (baby)Shutterstock/Yu Zhang (fox)jimkruger/Getty Images **L156 Side 01** (gull)akz ©123RF.com **L157 Side 01** (frame)C Squared Studios/Getty Images (man)NicolasMcComber/E+/Getty Images (feathers)Geza Farkas/123RF (baby)Kwame Zikomo/Purestock/SuperStock **L158 Side 02** (apple)Shutterstock/baibaz **L158 Side 03** (beach/ocean)Glow Images/Superstock (fly)arlindo71/Getty Images (kittens)leoba/123RF (police)©Hill Street Studios/Blend Images LLC (baseball player)Shutterstock/Peter Weber (hole)©McGraw-Hill Education (diving)Vendla Stockdale/Shutterstock (beach)©iStockphoto.com/fallbrook (feathers)Juj Winn/Moment/Getty Images **L159 Side 03** (sea turtle)Kjeld Friis .dk/Getty Images (whale)James R.D. Scott/Getty Images (goldfish)Anthony Bradshaw/Getty Images (flour)belchonock/123RF (seals)pilipenkod ©123RF.com (shark)Shutterstock/Thomas Duerrenberger (snake)Madele/Shutterstock (bread)Everyday Images/Alamy **MT16 Side 01** (beans)Maxim Tatarinov/123RF (seed in soil)serezniy/123RF (seedling)Peter Lewis/123RF (rice plant)Korradol Yamsattham/123RF (wheat seedlings)Leonid Eremeychuk/123RF **MT16 Side 02** (corn ear)YinYang/Getty Images (corn stalk)Pixtal/age footstock (wheat field)Bear Dancer Studios/Mark Dierker (wheat seeds)McGraw-Hill Education/Jacques Cornell (flour)belchonock/123RF